Chemo On The Rocks:
My Great Alaskan Misadventure

By Rebecca L. Durkin

Chemo On The Rocks:
My Great Alaskan Misadventure

by: Rebecca L. Durkin

Published by
Christine F. Anderson Publishing & Media, Madison VA, 22727
www.publishwithcfa.com

CHRISTINE F. ANDERSON
PUBLISHING & MEDIA

ISBN: 978-0692299494

Printed in the United States of America

Reviews

Original and touching, this true story in the Northwest and Alaska makes you fall in love with the author. Nothing prepares you for the impact of the invisible monster of ovarian cancer on this tenaciously energetic young woman. Her talent in seeing the humor in everyday situations, as well as during the horrific, makes this book a "must read."

Kathleen Shaputis, author, ghostwriter

Chemo on the Rocks wasn't like reading any other book; I found myself walking, living and breathing right alongside of the Becky. This author details her images with such texture and the story lines with such realness it is as though you are living the experience with her. It is a prodigious read that caused me to often contemplate, laugh and experience the truth of how life's ebb and flow shapes our existence. Ms. Durkin grabs your hand from the beginning as you feel the forward rush of things ahead—only to land back on earth— forever changed in how you view medicine, miracles and your own life's misadventures.

Tracy J Covington, Ph.D., BCB, AAPM
Licensed Clinical Psychologist

Chemo on the Rocks is not just a story about the turmoil, pain, and suffering of a cancer patient, but a story of how she maintained with courage and a "pick up your boot straps and forge ahead with a smile" attitude, which is an inspirational testimony.

Beverly Seibold

An authentically written story about the author's courageous journey through her life and battle with cancer. An inspiring story for anyone whose life has been touched by personal illness.

Jennifer Hughey

Table of Contents

Other Books by the Author

Behind the Smile—a short story in the anthology titled *Suffer the Women* by Wilfried Lippman.

Dedication

For Mom and Dad, Rick, Jeffrey and MacKenzie

"Against the assault of laughter nothing can stand." Mark Twain

"There is a thin line that separates laughter and pain, comedy and tragedy, humor and hurt." Erma Bombeck

"It's always something." Gilda Radner

Acknowledgements

A special thank you to Kathleen Shaputis, whose gentle encouragement and loving advice kept me writing when I was ready to give up, and Tracy Covington who gave me a platform to express myself. They pushed me further than I ever thought I could go. Their encouragement was the impetus for finally finishing my book.

I especially want to thank my favorite readers; Lynne Chesley, Skie Bender, Jane Brooks, Nancy Govaars, Nikki Julien, Jody Bellanich, Beverly Seibold, Jennifer Hughey, and Elaine Canary, for taking the time to read my book and provide valuable feedback.

Thank you Bonnie Alsup-Sullivan for making me laugh, and for taking my picture for the book cover.

Thank you Mom and Dad for molding my quirky sense of humor, and for all the love and support a daughter could ever wish to receive, and Mike and Curt for allowing me to share stories about them.

Mike McCormick was by my side during some of the most difficult times of my life. Special thanks to him for allowing me to share stories about our time together.

Jeffrey and MacKenzie have lived with a distracted writer mom for years. Thank you Jeffrey for accompanying me on the long drives to writer's meetings, and MacKenzie for providing all kinds of fun things to write about.

Thank you Christine Anderson for publishing my story and for being so great to work with, and for reminding me that I am a survivor and that I should "own it!"

This book would not have been born without my husband's suggestion to gather the poems I'd scribbled on sticky notes and use them as an outline for my story. His recognition that I had something to say brought my story to life. Thank you Rick for your loving support of my writing for the last two decades.

Special thanks to the Ovarian Cancer National Alliance for allowing me to partner with them and to spread the word about the important work they do. It is my pleasure to share book sale proceeds towards such a worthy cause.

Foreword

Becky (Rebecca) has always had a different path. When I first met her we were students at Lutheran Bible Institute (LBI), a super seminary offering degrees in ministry and worship. Our friendship was a quick connect as we found ourselves often looking around at our fellow students, wondering how we had ever arrived at such a place. Becky, at the time, unbeknownst to either of us, was sick—very sick. It didn't present as cancer but a sleep sickness. She was tired ALL the time. I feel the tickle of regret thinking back at how gently she always acknowledged my ongoing commentary regarding her life emphasis to sleep. Tired she was, yet her soft depth and whimsical mischief fortified my adoration of her as we grew our adventures in friendship. We would "snickle" (our term for our muffled laugh that wanted to take flight but didn't dare due to our sobering surroundings) often at our observations and encounters; our days were textured and colorful as we resided in a restored convent. Our dorm rooms were the remnants of nun cubbies. Stunningly special and surprisingly quirky was our friendship together as our surroundings unfolded in a year of life-discovery.

We both departed after one year at LBI; I returned to Seattle and Becky to Ketchikan, but we quickly reconnected as housemates in the "UW district." I was attending University of Washington and Becky came following my invitation to get a fresh start after a challenging relationship. We made the best of our limited time between my extensive student hours and her challenge at finding a job in a college town without a car. We loved our housemate days although they came to a close rather rapidly. We said our goodbyes when Becky relinquished the possibility of steady work and returned home. I missed her greatly but continued in my own overwhelmed student status as I prepared to finish my undergraduate degree and hurriedly find my place in graduate school.

Our lives separated and parted…there were many years without contact. Phone calls identified our new lives as married women—with careers unfolding—and cancer. Our lives separated again, for more than two decades, until a Facebook message arrived on

June 19, 2011: a big hello and friend request from Rebecca! As we chatted with many words to catch up our pasts, I quickly understood that cancer had continued to be the centerpiece to her life. Yet, in Becky style, she had turned nightmarish days into meaning. Her extensive dossier of daunting medical providers, surgeries and crazy chemotherapy was a wicked story that only halted somewhat in the face of birthing her first child followed by relational catastrophes and structural life changes. She triumphed as she remarried and had a second child, both children, modern miracles. In this time…across all the blows of life, Becky's writing became her solace, her sanity and her best friend.

I was emotionally breathless when we began our sharings of what we had been doing with our "wild" lives. It was June and I was preparing for my third annual Women's Retreat. It was uncanny to discover that she had published part of her memoirs in the book "Suffer the Women." Uncanny because I had been searching Amazon, Google and my bookshelves for a book of short stories where women had stretched…and overcame the hooks of life. The book was perfect for what my needs were, why hadn't I found it? It was out of print. Sigh. Alas, Becky was able to tap her connections to find not only one copy of the book, but enough to provide a copy to every woman who attended my weekend retreat! Reading her story in print was intoxicating. Her writing, a mix of satire, warm humor and psychological prickliness, manifested in tears spilling off my face as I laughed, wept and viscerally felt the pulse of her life ebb and flow.

As we found our old groove and new-flavored friendship, I woke up one night to the vision of her reading her memoirs to the women attending the October 2012 retreat. It would be our first reunion in over 25 years and would require her to travel from her home in Washington to mine, in California.

The plan was cemented and I remember…like it was a moment ago, picking her up at the airport. Her tiny frame and big-embracing eyes were as always…only the fashion had changed, and there we were. That year, she sat in a white rocking chair, with side table and lamp, as she read sections of her memoirs to 30 retreaters. It was spellbinding...and everything manifested from perfect potentialities! There she was—my long ago-sleepy friend who had awakened the fire within, transcended the turbulence by flying higher and with love and deep willingness brought her message, her purpose, to teach others to overcome.

It's 2014 and this will be Becky's third year to teach at my fifth annual Women's Retreat. We expect double the attendees as she has become a favorite, a Cancer Rock Star, who teaches us crazy, creative ways to manifest LIFE and memorialize our paths. In her presence we all become writers of our story. Robust and resilient, her presence grows as I have watched from the sidelines; my once "snickly" and fragile friend has shifted into a leviathan of powerful truth. Her message, her meaning, and her purpose are the same—to reduce suffering in others, to encourage from a place of knowledge, and to embody the story that WE were all meant to be... the vastness of transcendence.

Tracy J Covington, Ph.D., BCB, AAPM

Licensed Clinical Psychologist

COO – Bickford, Covington & Associates

Introduction

Chemo on the Rocks
My Great Alaskan Misadventure

Sticks and stones may break my bones, but words will never hurt me.

When my doctors uttered the words Cancer, Chemotherapy, Oophorectomy, and Survivor, I had proof the saying wasn't true. Those words stung. They echoed for years. They affected not just me, but everyone who loved me.

Everyone has a unique reaction to the word Cancer. Some people start planning for their death, some live a terror-filled life, and some are humbled. When I heard Stage III Ovarian Carcinoma, I had a few choice words of my own and death was not one of them.

I have had an uneasy relationship with the word "survivor" and I am uncomfortable with the label. I won't bear the burden of a gold survivor medal, signifying I won the contest—no flaws, no mistakes—but I'll proudly claim an honorable mention for a round well fought.

I've logged multiple laps around the IV gauntlet and hunkered down in the fallopian trenches. I've had two children in defiance of a cancerous beast and fought an epic battle on the front lines of the Hormone War Zone in Meno Meno Land, all while trying to weather Ketchikan, Alaska's thirteen feet of annual precipitation that saturated the wig on my head.

I'd like to believe my *survival* had something to do with my attitude. I didn't create a bucket list of must-do's before death, and I didn't vow to eat healthy and exercise in penance for being denied entry through the pearly gates. I just continued to muddle along in spite of the debilitating diagnosis, hiding behind a permanent smile, letting very few people see the cracks in my façade.

Chapter 1

Short toddler legs and sharp driftwood slivers slowed me down as I tried to keep up with my older brother Mike as he hopped from log to log in front of our Whidbey Island home. Snow-capped Mount Baker loomed high in the distance, completing the backdrop of our postcard existence. Lazy summer days sipping lemonade with neighbors, playing with cousins and friends, and a friendly black lab named Sam proved the American dream.

Dad's store, Bill's Jiffy Mart, was just a few miles away in downtown Oak Harbor. Clad in his green apron, he spent hours arranging perfect rows of canned vegetables and fruit. He always had a pencil tucked behind his ear, a feather duster in his hand, and a pen in the pocket protector of his crisp white shirt. There was nothing better than leaning into the freezer and pulling a crystalized Fudgesicle on a sunny day or trying to decide which box of Cracker Jacks had the best prize. I loved the store and all the promotional gimmicks Dad brought home, like my life-sized green Squirt soda balloon with fuzzy hair, and the greatest prize of all, my bright red two-seated tricycle.

Bill's Jiffy Mart had a small home in the back parking lot. When I was about three we left the beach to live closer to the store, substituting convenient downtown living for fresh salty air. We moved from picture-perfect postcard to a postage stamp lot. A public beach was not far from our home but repeated pestering didn't sway Mom to drive me there any sooner.

Impatient to play in the water, I planned our beach escape for days. "Hurry up, Sam," I lisped, as we furiously dug a hole under the fence. We belly-crawled under the fence and I loaded Sam into my powder blue get-away wagon. I tugged at my swimsuit trying to loosen the itchy dirt, as my canine conspirator and I began our trek. Sam's pink tongue dripped with excitement as I pulled him across the parking lot. I had plans to show Sam Oak Harbor's Flintstone-mobile and for a dip in City Beach Lagoon, which would wash away all evidence of our escape. We made it all the way to the end of the parking lot and hung a left towards the beach.

"Becky! Sam!" Mom's voice, shrill above the busy traffic, brought everything to an abrupt halt. Sam abandoned me on the side of the road and went skulking back to Mom as she bustled across the parking lot. The whole town heard my wails as she spanked me in front of the busy intersection, loaded my downtrodden dog and me into the wagon, and pulled us back to my backyard prison. My tears stained the brown floor tiles inside Bill's Jiffy Mart as Mom reported my crime to Dad. After careful consideration, he gave me a Canada Dry Ginger Ale, his feather duster, and put me to work in the canned goods section.

A year or so later we'd outgrown our humble abode behind the store and moved to a larger home with a neighborhood filled with friends for Mike and me. Mike had a tree house high up in a backyard tree, with a strategically absent rung to keep his sister from infiltrating the fort. Sam had free run on the grassy lawn, and I spent hours playing hide and seek in the forest just beyond our property line. My all-time favorite activity was pushing my two-seater trike to the top of the hill for the exhilarating ride back down, stopping only by the skin of my shoes. I got in big trouble from a friend's mother when her daughter hopped on behind me and set her barefoot brakes—Fred Flintstone style.

As our house size grew, so did our family and Mom's tummy expanded by the minute. A tiny baby was getting ready to join the Holman clan, and I had plans for my new sister. I would dress her up in fluffy dresses and push her around the neighborhood in my doll stroller. I was anxious to have a real live doll and after what seemed like forever the big day finally arrived. Dad drove Mom across

Deception Pass Bridge to the hospital in Anacortes, while Mike and I stayed home with Grandma Chesley.

It seemed Mom had been gone for days. When the phone jangled, I pounced at the first ring.

"Hello?"

"We have a new baby."

"What's her name?"

"Curt."

It took a minute before the meaning behind the name dawned on me. How could Mom ruin my months of planning in one phone call? There was nothing more to say, so I hung up on her and tried to figure out what I'd do with a baby brother.

Curt grew from a robust baby to a darling brown-eyed imp whose summertime tans set off his shaggy blond hair, and even though he shunned pink dresses, he was a fun playmate. In contrast, Mom says I was puny. I had straight brown helmet hair, deep blue eyes, colorless lips, a crooked smile, freckles, knobby knees, and a lisp. I wanted long pigtails with ribbons, but Mom had no desire to fight my fine locks. Every few months she drove her stringy-haired daughter to downtown Oak Harbor for a visit to the beauty parlor where purple-tinged, pin-curled Betty and Evelyn waited for their next victim. Permanent wave solution and cigarette smoke burned my nose as I turned page after page of glossy picture books and smiled back at the little girls sporting beautiful curls. The pink-smocked gals gently set the impossible styles aside, pulled out a black padded bench, laid it over the salon chair, and pumped it up to haircut height. Betty attempted to hold me while Evelyn wielded scissors dangerously close to my ears, promising me a lollipop if I held still. I jumped out of the chair as a Peter Pan pixie. I loved the pink ladies. I hated the haircuts.

Afterwards Mom tried to make amends for my hair loss with a trip to the shoe store next door. Mousy locks for Mary Janes. My hair looked ridiculous but my feet were always well-clad.

I endured stupid haircuts well into grade school, but my pixie looks were not a problem when Clover Valley Elementary School cast me to deliver the leading line in the Spring Concert. Our first grade class had been practicing silly barnyard songs for weeks. On the evening of the big event, Mom pinned a giant blue bow to my slippery locks, completely dwarfing my head. The tiny singers passed the microphone around as the bevy of children bellowed a barnyard bleat, moo or quack, much to the delight of their proud parents. At the end of each animal utterance, I stood tall at the center microphone and belted out *And the Cat Goeth Fiddle I Fee*. I was confused when the entire audience roared each time I sang my part. Whether because they thought I was adorable in my oversized bow and pronounced lisp, or hilarious, I'll never know, but my blue bow sunk lower behind the students after each *Fiddle I Fee*.

Stormy Seas

Our new home was a short drive from the bluffs high atop the Strait of Juan de Fuca, where trees bow inland over fertile land—a backwards genuflection to the powerful sea. Mom enjoyed packing her brood in the car and driving us to West Beach, a perfect vantage point to view crashing waves. The temperate wind blew up the sleeves of my navy blue windbreaker and whipped through Mom's sheer floral scarf as she sat on a log and kept close tabs on Curt. Mike and I discovered glittery mica embedded in massive rocks, climbed around the driftwood under eroding bluffs, and shouted above the pounding noise of the sea.

One day the coastal winds built to a powerful storm that threw branches and debris around our neighborhood. Mom, Curt and I came back from town to find huge uprooted fir trees, like giant Lincoln Logs, scattered on the lawn. Realizing Mike wasn't in the house, Mom looked out the window to see his tree fort was intact, but there was no sign of him in the swaying fortress. She was starting to panic when she glimpsed a note on the kitchen counter:

Mother dear, I am not here, but do not fear, I have my football helmet on.

4

Mike eventually emerged from the woods clad in his protective headgear. The world in all of its powerful glory could be a scary place for a mother with three young children.

Sickbay

I had fears too, especially of needle-wielding nurses. Mom planned a fun mother-daughter outing without the boys, but I was unaware of the scheduled detour to visit my pediatrician. Mom and I chatted easily on the way to Anacortes —as soon as we'd cleared the scary Deception Pass Bridge—the link between the mainland and Whidbey Island.

The easy chatter dissipated as soon as the doctor set down his stethoscope and mentioned the word "shot." I could not sit on the examining table with the huge bright light in my face and allow them to poke my arm. I climbed off the table and squirmed and flinched and squealed. My mother and the nurse agreed with me that the pain would be no more than a bee's sting, which didn't sound so bad until I remembered the last time I stepped on a bee while running through the sprinkler. I started flailing my arms in an animated anxiety attack. Mom suggested we take a walk and told the clinic staff she'd bring me back soon.

We walked to a park where I spied numerous piles of brown crusty puff mushrooms. I hopped from cluster to cluster watching the yellow smoke emanating from decimated fungi. It was so fun I urged Mom to try. She found herself a perfectly preserved pile and brought her shoe down hard on an unfortunate mound of slippery slimy doggy doo. Mom slid her foot around in the grass trying to remove the evidence as I doubled-over in laughter. We were still laughing when the doctor shot me in the arm, which didn't seem near as bad as what Mom had to go through.

We spent a fair amount of time at clinics for one mishap or another. Mike was involved in a school skirmish one afternoon and suffered a concussion. Earlier that week Curt climbed onto the arm of the brown over-stuffed rocking chair to play our strictly prohibited game of spinning to Japan. We giggled excitedly as I spun the chair faster and faster. Curt went airborne, flew halfway around the world, and crash-landed on the hearth, which landed me a crashing whack with the wooden spoon. When Mom drove up to the clinic door to unload Mike, Curt tried to escape the moving vehicle, eager to avoid the doctor who'd treated his broken collarbone. Dad's pragmatic approach to the problem was to remove the inside handles from the backseat of the Pontiac. I spent years sandwiched between my two brothers after that, and all attempts at escape were futile.

I didn't suffer broken bones or accidents warranting trips to ER. My conditions were subtle. One vaccination day I missed school and Mom had to drive me all the way to the health clinic in Coupeville to get my Rubella booster, which beat standing in line with hundreds of school kids for humiliating height and weight checks, followed by a painful shot in the arm. I laughed in relief when I didn't even feel the needle, but when I mentioned the room was spinning and turning black, the nurse loaded me into an official looking station wagon and drove Mom and me to the hospital. I'd had a mild reaction but I recall Mom's reaction was panicked. I also routinely tested positive to the tuberculosis tine test. I have never had TB but had to prove it each time with chest x-rays, which always warranted another trip to the clinic.

I frequently had nagging stomachaches or fatigue. The remedy was hanging out with compassionate school nurses. Lying down on the cool padded benches and playing a doctored version of pickup sticks with tongue depressors, often eased my tummy troubles. Sweet elementary school nurses doling out orange flavored baby aspirin foreshadowed oncology nurses pumping me full of poisons, and the journey between was, at times, long and arduous.

As accidents and anomalies became more frequent, fears began to dictate Mom's actions. She had always been terrified of Deception Pass Bridge, our closest exit off the island, but now a sharp intake of breath, and warnings about terrible dangers, accompanied my every move when hiking too near an edge, trying to outrun waves, or pedaling my trike too fast down the hill. At first, I scoffed at her fears. When Dad brought my beautiful blue Schwinn Cruiser home for my seventh birthday, I pushed it to the top of the hill and soared down, jumping on my pedal brakes at the last second and skidding into the driveway. But fear is insidious. It lurked in dark corners of my imagination, awaiting its chance to take residence in my mind where it flourished well beyond Mom's original anxieties.

Safe Harbor

The first time I recall seeing my mom cry was a quiet morning in 1968. She was stirring oatmeal and had just turned on the radio when she shushed me. A man named Bobby Kennedy had died. Mom sunk to a heap on the floor and began to wail. A hush settled on our household and on the neighborhood. Parents on the street spoke in hushed tones and there was an eerie pall on Loerland Lane.

Clover Valley Elementary was right next to the Whidbey Naval Air Station Base. The school bus passed the base every day, but my civilian status meant the base was off limits to me—except on special occasions when dads came home from a strange sounding place called Vietnam. On those occasions, bands played, mothers cried, and dads scooped up their kids and smothered them in kisses.

A girlfriend's family took me to a wondrous store called the Navy Exchange at the Seaplane Base in Oak Harbor. The Exchange had every toy imaginable. Boxes and boxes of Baby First Step, Hi Heidi, and Shrinking Violet taunted me from shelves just beyond my reach. The greatest prize of all—the Easy Bake Oven—was just waiting for a little girl like me to take it home and bake miniature cakes.

Our family had recently moved down the hill about five houses south and it wasn't long before my parents opened a bigger and better version of Bill's Jiffy Mart. In celebration of the grand opening, the store was festooned with celebratory bunting to welcome folks to the big event. Customers helped themselves to individually wrapped roasted peanuts and other goodies that overflowed brand new garbage cans. I stuffed myself with peanuts and helped myself to goodies from the shelves, but none of that activity could rival the visions of the Easy Bake Oven that invaded my daydreams. I couldn't wait to delight my family with delicacies prepared in my bedroom bakery.

I had a bad case of flu-based delirium on Christmas Eve and the brightly colored boxes of wonder taunted me from under the tinseled tree. Dad opened the Bible and began reading about shepherds, wise men, and Baby Jesus, as I lay next to the fireplace playing with the pixie elves I'd pulled from overstuffed stockings. After an eternity, it was time to open presents. While Curt ripped open his package, I could almost smell tasty treats as visions of cinnamon rolls danced in my head. When it was my turn, I tore through smiling snowman faces, reached in the box and pulled out…a miniature sewing machine. In my utter confusion, I said thank you for my "Easy Bake Sewing Machine" and attempted to pretend all was well in Beckyland, but seriously, who gives a sewing machine to a wannabe baker?

Someone made a big mistake at the North Pole, but I wasn't about to complain and ruin whatever chance was left of my remaining gifts. I pulled a small stuffed doll from my stocking that had a happy face on one side and a sad face on the other, perfectly capturing my feelings. I sat quietly befuddled as the rest of the family exchanged oohs and aahs about exciting new treasures.

A knock on the door broke my silence and I padded over to see who was on the porch.

When what to my wondering eyes should appear but the neighbor lady grinning ear to ear. Swaddled deep in her arms I glimpsed sight of white paws and a black curly puppy brought my own oohs and aahs.

My sickness and heartbreak over Christmas-gone-wrong dissipated the moment "Slippers" landed in my arms.

Slippers willingly participated in my games. I dressed him in petticoats, wrapped him in baby blankets and rocked him to sleep in my doll cradle. He followed me everywhere and nestled under my covers to warm my toes every night.

Glub, Glub, Glub

On the last day of second grade, classmates flashed big toothy grins as they skipped one-by-one to the front of the class, eager to retrieve their report cards and candy bar. It was the beginning of summer fun after an exhausting year of reading, writing, and arithmetic. I waited anxiously at my desk, certain my beloved teacher had saved the best for last. When all the kids were gone, I noticed my mother tiptoeing into the classroom. Happy about her unexpected appearance, I took her hand and led her to the front of the room; I pointed out the terrarium of little green frogs who croaked the Pledge of Allegiance with us every morning.

My teacher handed me my candy bar and asked Mom and me to take a seat. I slipped behind a desk as Mom tried to find a comfortable position in a miniature chair. The conversation went something like this:

"Rebecca."

"Yeth, Mithuth Rector."

"Your mother and I have decided to hold you back."

I shook my head. "Hold what?"

Mom explained. "We decided to hold you back. You need to stay in second grade."

I started screaming, "No. No. No!"

I flunked second grade—the absolute worst fate for a kid. Did they have any idea what happens on the playground to flunkers?

Becky flunked second grade, Becky flunked second grade, ha ha ha ha ha!

I sobbed in the backseat of the Pontiac and dreaded facing the rest of my family. When we got home, I ran to my room and hid with Slippers, soaking his curls with my tears as I told him all about my terrible day.

It was no consolation to learn it wasn't all my fault. A trip to the eye doctor revealed why I had trouble learning. When you've never seen with clarity you have no idea what it's like to see clearly, so I hadn't complained. My first pair of light blue, cat-eye glasses revealed the existence of the big "E" across the room. Letters took on new life as words like Spot, Sally, Dick and Jane formed before my eyes, adding new meaning to the picture stories. Unfortunately, my newfound sight didn't come in time to save me from my flunking fate.

Chapter 2

We moved to another school district on the island that summer, sparing me the indignity of facing my classmates when school started again. Our new home was on Strawberry Point, on a high bluff with a beautiful view of Camano Island.

Mom ruled the household and was especially conscientious about our new home. She could tell in a second if anyone had been in her room, used the good towels, sat on her bed, or sampled her perfumes, guaranteeing a good scolding. Hands and feet had no business on coffee tables and everything always looked immaculate. The house had two full stories. Upstairs was the formal dining and living room and bedrooms for my parents and Curt. Downstairs was kid and pet domain. My room came furnished with a red roll-top desk, vanity, and a pink and white gingham tufted bed—the perfect size for Slippers, my doll collection, and me. Mike's room came with a beautiful golden collie named Charlie. They shared their subterranean room at the back of the house, with only a small window to vent the smell of model paint and glue. Fighter jets hung from the ceiling and small jars of paint and dozens of brushes lined Mike's desk where he proudly displayed his prized model sailing vessel, the Cutty Sark.

After spending the summer getting used to our new digs, I was excited to start my new school with a clean slate, but some Sunday school snots were keeping score. They decided that since I didn't get to advance to third grade at school, then I should not advance in Godly activities either. The ringleader stood on the table and made the startling announcement in front of the entire class. Raucous laughter and jeers erupted from the boys as my girlfriends giggled. There was no sign of God in the room that day as I glowered at the roomful of rapscallions. The indignity of failing at school followed me up the church steps and into the sanctuary, while the background music in my head played a mournful ostracism dirge.

Devil to Pay

I wasn't sorry to leave the Sunday school hellions when my folks, no longer satisfied with the Lutheran liturgy, traded tradition for chaos by joining the charismatic movement of proud proselytizing Pentecostals. Adults raised their arms toward heaven, swayed back and forth, and wept openly.

When my parents began hosting prayer meetings, the weirdest people came to our house. I should have been downstairs playing with my dolls, but what happened upstairs was too entertaining to ignore. Quiet as a church mouse, I tiptoed into the room full of people and sat next to Mom at the base of her yellow floral chair. As Mom absentmindedly twisted my tufts into knots, I bore witness to stories, prayer requests, and miracles, but the stories I paid the most attention to weren't the *Jesus Loves Me This I Know* type. They were tales of evil books that shrieked when thrown in the fire or messages hand-delivered by Satan's manipulation of the Ouija Board. The room buzzed as people spoke in tongues, and spirit-filled, good Christian folk cast demons into the underworld, via our basement, right past my bedroom.

Entertainment upstairs turned to fear when I was alone at night. I was sure demons lay in wait for me to sleep so they could drag me to hell. My nightly prayer, *Now I lay me down to sleep, I pray the Lord my soul to keep, thy love guard me through the night and wake me with the morning light*, did little to ease my terror. Slippers and I nearly suffocated under my pink quilted bedspread as we waited for daylight, where demons refused to play.

Demons aside, I loved being a country kid living not too far away from town. We had wide-open spaces to play with the dogs; an ornery horse named Topper to ride, and Kitty, our independent cat.

The raspberry bushes bordering the backyard were full of foot-long brown garter snakes, which Charlie whipped around like frayed rope. I swung high into the trees on the tire swing and sometimes we could carefully walk down the steep trail to the beach far below. Adding to Mom's anxiety about heights and other unforeseen disasters, Curt constantly disappeared on explorations for elusive toads and lizards.

One sunny afternoon I jumped off the school bus and found Mom sitting on a stump in the horse field with a deflated pink hair dryer bonnet on her head. The dogs ran circles around her and Topper hovered ominously as she wailed about her missing boy. Dad arrived just as our young explorer emerged from the woods—pockets bulging with treasures—oblivious to any danger. Curt had great faith and few worries. He was certain if he fell from the bluff, the angels would catch him and deliver him safely back home. Apparently, he'd been eavesdropping on the prayer meetings too. Curt flew with angels while I hid from devils.

Merrily, Merrily—Life Is But a Dream

My second attempt at second grade was much better than my first. My teacher was a grandmotherly Dutch woman who invited me to her farmhouse for tea and cookies. She worked hard at boosting my confidence and wrote in my report card that I was twice as smart as I thought I was. She sent me to speech therapy to work on my "lazy s's" which were even more pronounced because of the retainer I wore to correct my crooked smile. She also enrolled me in a speed-reading program. Soon piles of paperbacks cluttered my nightstand. I never even had to leave my room to enjoy adventures far beyond our island shoreline.

Curiously, while I lived vicarious adventures through storybooks from under the warmth of my covers, my doctor diagnosed me as hyperactive. It's possible I exhibited some hyper energy while trying to avoid a shot in the bottom, but I don't recall ever being described as having too much energy. Nevertheless, he prescribed a magic orange pill, guaranteed to calm any restlessness. I floated on a mellow fluffy cloud like a seagull on a windy day. Poof!—from chatterbox to subdued and submissive, I was the perfect little girl. But the hyper antidote could be tricky.

It hit me during the windmill exercises in PE, the ones where you are supposed to touch your foot with the opposite hand, and if you have an ounce of coordination, you would look right at home in a field of tulips in Amsterdam. Suddenly everything was in slow motion. My arms floated above my head. Left hand, left ear? Right hand, left elbow? The low titter in the gym became a thunderous roar as my classmates laughed at my circus act. The school nurse escorted me to her office to await my mother. No one dialed O for Operator or rushed me to a hospital to get my stomach pumped, or whatever one does when dealing with an adverse side effect. No, Mom and her friend Sue tapped my quirky upper/downer energy for a day of power shopping in Seattle. I lay down unfettered on the back seat, eavesdropped on church gossip, and recovered just fine.

After the windmill incident, Mom chucked the pills. With the absence of hyper-inhibitors, I became a champ on the monkey bars and won running races at school. I also found better things to do than floating on a sea of bubbles in the tub. Choosing cruising over bathing, I snuck into the garage, jumped on my blue bicycle, pedaled as fast as I could from one end of the driveway to the other, and landed on my face. I broke my glasses, my retainer, and a front tooth. My eardrums nearly burst as Mom and the dentist both took their turns yelling at me.

I smiled behind masking tape covered glasses in my school photo that year, my insubordination captured for eternity, and all the work in speech therapy was for naught, now that I had a snaggle tooth to snare my lazy s's.

Mini-dramas and tummy aches notwithstanding, life was good. I enjoyed slumber parties with girlfriends, swimming in the lagoon at City Beach, and Bluebird Day Camp at Deception Pass Park, where I could hike the trails above the Pass, away from Mom's constant worry. Our relatives were scattered about the state and we often had fun get-togethers.

Preferring organ music to banging drums, my parents did a Lutheran U-turn and walked the red carpet right back to their comfortable pew. The girls accepted me back into the fold and the mean Sunday school boys moved on to another hapless victim. Being Lutheran again meant I would be able to spend a week at Lutherwood church camp at Samish Lake as soon as I was old enough. Lutherwood filled me with as much wonder as an enchanted theme park, and I couldn't wait for my turn there to sing Kumbaya, and roast marshmallows by the campfire.

School was going well too. I had two best friends to twirl around the monkey bars with at recess and a couple of cute boys kept me entertained with playground shenanigans. On top of all that, my classmates at Crescent Harbor Elementary voted me Best Citizen of the Fourth Grade.

Why'd They Have to Rock the Boat?

I started fifth grade still basking in my Best Citizen status. I had a beautiful teacher who read to us every day. All the kids hovered round as page-by-page she introduced us to *James and the Giant Peach*.

Things were going so well for me I'd been unaware of financial troubles on the home front and I couldn't believe it when my parents announced we were moving. We weren't loading up the Pontiac for a quick move across town, and we weren't moving five houses south. We were heading north to a faraway land called Ketchikan, Alaska.

Moving seemed like a ridiculous idea, but I soon learned not everything revolved around me. I'd missed clues, like the salvaged fabric scattered under Mom's sewing machine. I'd been impressed as she stitched stylish creations for me instead of our yearly shopping spree to Mount Vernon. I felt so stylish in my blue plaid maxi dress and brown wool poncho with pom-poms that matched Mom's jumper.

Dad said he had a new job at a grocery store in Ketchikan. He hung up his apron, packed his bachelor kit, and left Whidbey Island for a foreign Alaskan shore 650 miles away. Mom stayed behind to pack up our life. I'm sure she'd never shopped a garage sale and now she was forced to hold one of her own. Hundreds of people rummaged our possessions. The garage sale was supposed to be— in the garage—but obnoxious strangers wandered through our house, upstairs and downstairs, poking their noses into all the nooks and crannies. My red two-seater trike and blue getaway wagon rolled out of my life forever, and my treasured, pink tufted double bed left with the highest bidder.

Mike deemed his model collection unlikely to survive the move. One-by-one, he threw them in the air like skeet and blasted them with a shotgun, saving them from a dishonorable death at the landfill.

We stowed our remaining possessions in the moving van and said goodbye to our pets. Topper trotted off to another hayfield, and strangers drove away with Kitty and Charlie.

Chapter 3

The M/V Wickersham sank a bit lower under the weight of my sorrows, as Mom drove the Pontiac onto the car deck.

It was a nippy October day and people hurried topside to stow their belongings, or stand at the rail to bid a fond farewell to Seattle before the chilly wind chased them back inside. The ship's crew tossed the lines, severing our tether to Washington, as the smokestack blared our departure. The captain set a course for the multi-day voyage via the Inside Passage from Washington through British Columbia and on up to Southeast Alaska.

I had to leave my precious cargo, Slippers, on the oily car deck, shivering and scared, instead of stowing him in my warm stateroom bunk. Between visits to feed my forlorn pooch, we explored the ship from aft to bow tiptoeing between backpacks and passengers sprawled out on the floor in sleeping bags.

The Wickersham was a beautiful ship with friendly pursers eager to share information about Alaska. Under the warmth of heated yellow lights, the solarium offered views of soaring eagles, swooping seagulls, and jagged coastline. We enjoyed succulent salmon and flaky halibut in the formal dining room, but my sadness was overwhelming in spite of the ship's pleasures.

We officially entered Alaska when we sailed into Dixon Entrance and my sadness about the move slowly yielded to anticipation.

Land Ho

The Wickersham sailed into the Tongass Narrows at pre-dawn and we saw the sparkling city lights of Ketchikan for the first time. Illuminated, the city looked large as we quietly sailed into port.

Bleary-eyed Dad greeted his stir-crazy family at the dock. We were excited to see him, and we followed him to our new home, just up the hill about five minutes away. Home was a three-story structure, boasting an endless view, but overcast skies kept it shrouded in mystery for days. When the sun finally melted the clouds, we had our first glimpse of snow-dusted mountains and the black Tongass Narrows. Wide-open nature beckoned outside, but no privacy existed between the rice-paper thin walls of the apartment building, and cooking smells wafted from one unit to the other. Mike and Curt stumbled over large waffle stompers and tripped on small army men before drawing an imaginary line of demarcation down the middle of their shared room. My bedroom window opened onto the public deck. Neighbors clomped up and down the steps until the wee hours, which kept Slippers agitated all night.

Daylight revealed Ketchikan was smaller than its twinkling lights led me to believe. Situated on Revillagigedo Island—the 12th largest island in the United States—you can drive from one end of Tongass Highway to the other in about an hour. Once settled into our new home, we began to explore our surroundings. We took a spin through downtown where businesses dotted the waterfront of Tongass Narrows on one side of the road, and houses stair-stepped up the mountainside on the other. Many houses had no road access and people schlepped groceries, furniture, and building supplies up hundreds of steps like pack mules. Deer Mountain, at just over three thousand feet, cast deep shadows on the town below, and businesses jutted out over the water on wooden docks anchored by creosote pilings. We bounced over the wooden pilings on Water Street, high above the Tongass Narrows, and watched floatplanes landing amongst fishing boats in the busy harbor.

Another day we drove to the north end of the island. It took about 30 minutes to reach Settlers Cove, at the end of the road, a whole 18 miles away. At Settlers Cove, we stretched our legs and dodged the raindrops while enjoying the Tongass Rainforest for the first time. The misty forest displayed heathery greens and browns in the hues of hemlock, fir, and spruce. Lupine held perfect raindrops, and moss and lichen covered rocks and trees, like nature's blanket against the elements.

I was fascinated by brightly painted houses that appeared to be stuck in the mud at Mud Bight. Hours later the mud-stuck homes, floating just beyond the highway guardrail, gently bobbed on the tide, as wood smoke and lit windows showed signs of life. Just around the corner from Mud Bight, Totem Bight offered a walk among large totems and a photo op in the opening of the Clan House. We discovered more totem poles in Saxman Native Village, a couple miles south of downtown Ketchikan. Continuing our journey, we drove to the end of the pavement just eight miles south. Not believing this could be it, we continued a few more miles, dodging potholes on the gravel road before we came to the end. And this was it. We'd left one island rock and landed on another but this one had no easy escape to the mainland.

Galley Talk

We found refuge at Kay's Kitchen. Situated at the top of Bar Harbor, it offered warm respite to the fishermen below and reservations on Saturday morning were a must. Sometimes the line stretched out the door and down the street. No one seemed to mind that it was usually raining horizontally. Sauerkraut and pastrami emanated from the back door as, whiff by wonderful whiff, we inched closer to the entry. Water flowed from downspouts, soaking us a bit more, as we edged ever nearer the threshold and caught a glimpse of a mountainous peanut butter pie. People chattered as rain spattered, but once inside we'd hang up our waterlogged coats, catch up on a week's worth of gossip while enjoying a favorite sandwich, and watch fishing boats chug past the breakwater. Our visits there would become a weekly tradition spanning almost thirty years for Mom and me. Kay's special blend of friendship, flavor and fun offered a warm umbrella against the elements, and underneath we began to build Ketchikan camaraderie.

Dropping Anchor

Dad seemed content in his new position at a local grocery store and I don't recall him being particularly upset about our new life, but Mom's anguish was palpable. She'd left her lovely home and was not happy with her new accommodations. Her mood was as dark as the mist that hovered above the town. She sought solace in the bathroom—the only private space in the apartment—knitting us scarves for Christmas, and undoubtedly silently cursing the day the Wickersham left her marooned on the island.

Mike appeared to ease into his first year at Ketchikan High School (Kayhi). He had new friends, enjoyed Alaskan hunting and fishing adventures, and seemed to be getting along great. It seemed all boys 14 or older zoomed up and down Ketchikan's steep hills on motorcycles. Mike bought one shortly after we moved to Alaska and we were all furious when he found multiple holes poked into the seat by the vandals and pranksters who ruled the apartment building. One morning we opened our front door to find a bag of dog poop on our stoop. I'm not sure what the message was supposed to be, but it certainly didn't come from the Welcome Wagon.

Curt joined the apartment pranksters, and took great delight in playing with matches in front of the building. Shortly after our arrival in Ketchikan, I took him for a walk downtown. We wandered inside a hardware store toy area, splitting up to find our aisle of interest. Hearing a ruckus, I found the owner demanding Curt empty his pockets. I defended my brother, assuring the owner he must be mistaken, but he was insistent about my brother's guilt. I was stunned when Curt's pockets revealed rubber spiders, bouncing balls and marbles. My darling, towhead brother, looked like a thief from the set of Oliver Twist.

I made new friends in school and started a lucrative babysitting gig in the apartment building. I was just a kid myself, but no one seemed to mind.

Cold Water

With all of its hills, Ketchikan provided the perfect playground when the temperature dropped enough to turn chilly rain into fluffy snow. Jefferson and Madison Streets were excellent for sledding. Entire families joined in the fun, doubled up on wooden sleds, or spun in saucers, with scarfs flying and dogs happily barreling down alongside. Giant snow berms at the bottom usually kept sledders from careening into cars on Tongass Avenue.

The best Christmas gifts that year were ice skates for the family. When we heard Ward Lake was frozen we gathered blankets and thermoses and piled into the Pontiac. Sparkling trees heavy with silver thaw flanked the dirt road to the lake. Reluctant to let us skate too far out on the large lake and risk breaking through thin ice, Dad drove us back to a smaller pond to test drive our skates. Glittery snow crunched under our feet as we wobbled on thin blades to the shoveled skating area. My feet were as frozen as the spilt hot chocolate that froze instantly on my arm, but I spent hours bumbling on the pond, while experienced skaters practiced easy figure eights.

Down She Goes

The snow was always great fun but I appreciated not having a long morning trek to school through knee-deep muddy slush when it thawed. I got wet enough just walking to the elementary school across the street from our apartment. The playground had a huge open wigwam-type structure to keep kids dry during recess, but the wind carried the rain right on through, soaking us almost every single day. My beautiful plaid maxi-dress grew longer and heavier with every splash from a mud puddle.

I'd been so happy with my gentle storybook reading teacher on Whidbey Island. My new teacher was sarcastic and reminded me of a storybook giant. His favorite game was hoisting students over his shoulder and depositing them—headfirst—in the tall narrow metal garbage cans. Legs kicked and flailed to no avail. There was no escape from the green cylinders full of snot-encrusted tissues. Finally resurrected by their captor, students emerged from the can triumphant, their eyes rimmed in pencil shavings. I was fortunate to escape the ridiculous rite of passage, but I did not escape his mockery.

Concerned about my math scores, Mom wrote a note to my teacher about my need for extra help. Always ready to make a spectacle out of student, the giant leaned on the front of his desk and called the class to order. He pulled Mom's note from his breast pocket and announced he had a note from Rebecca's mother. He went on to read:

Rebecca is struggling with math. Please provide some after school help for her.

In a slow drawl, dripping in sarcasm, he went on to say something like:

She must not have learned anything in that school down south.

The class erupted in giggles, eerily similar to the second-grade flunking incident. My "down-south" schooling followed me up the Inside Passage and left me stranded at the feet of an ogre. In just five years, I'd failed a grade, redeemed myself the following year, was honored as the Best Citizen of the Fourth Grade, and demoted to not having learned anything. I slid down in my chair and tried to disappear.

Even Keel

The following year I was free from the sneers of an insensitive educator. My sixth grade teacher had an unconventional approach to teaching and I thrived in the environment he created. At the front of the classroom was the "living room" containing tattered, overstuffed and mismatched furniture where kids sprawled out and planned activities for the year. A back corner contained a darkroom where we learned to develop pictures. I loved picking up the plastic tongs and dipping photographic papers into the chemical baths that transformed them into a photo of a classmate.

Adding to the wonder, our classroom looked and smelled like a menagerie. Iguanas, gerbils, and white rats were always crawling up and over someone's head as we sat in our living room, planning our spring field trip.

With no hard link to the mainland, Ketchikan's field trips were always an adventure. Other than a short day-trip to a beach or Ward Lake a few miles away, the trips typically involved a ferry or plane ride. Our class planned a weeklong trip to Jasper, Alberta. We held fund-raisers and garage sales to raise money for our escapade. The parents of one of the students owned a shoe store and they donated several pairs for us to sell at our garage sale. Recognizing an opportunity to get rid of the hideous black boots with fake licorice laces that Mom bought me in preparation for our life in the rain, instead of the "impractical" granny boots I wanted, I ran across the street to our apartment and unburied them from the back of my closet. I gave Slippers a tickle behind his ears before I skipped back to school with the brand new boots, hoping they would end up on the feet of another unfortunate innocent. I was pleased to be able to make such a generous contribution to the field trip coffers. I don't know how Mom found out what I had done, but she donned her detective hat, found the buyer, and bought my ugly boots back. I skulked back home with my ugly boots and buried them even deeper in my closet.

Having raised enough money, our class boarded a ferry bound for Prince Rupert, BC. Dixon Entrance was not as welcoming as it had been when we sailed toward Ketchikan on the Wickersham. The ferry dived into gaping troughs, climbed back up mountainous crests, and pitched from side to side. It felt like we were at the mercy of a rambunctious boy scuttling toy boats in the bathtub. In my ignorant bliss—before my fears of deep cold water—I joined the kids who were using slippery seat cushions as sleds to ride the waves up and down the floor, while others suffered debilitating seasickness.

After spending an evening in Prince Rupert, BC, we hopped aboard a train for the trip to Jasper. I loved walking between the train cars and hearing the whoosh of the doors. Our teacher and chaperones were very patient with their brood of noisy and boisterous kids.

The mountains rose into the vibrant blue sky over the crispy clean town of Jasper, where I spent my field trip money on cheap souvenirs and candy. Our class stayed at a hostel where the din from excited sixth graders echoed off the Rockies and summoned the wildlife to take a closer look. A classmate was outside the hostel when a bear came barreling down the mountainside. We all yelled, "Bear! Bear!" The boy came running toward the hostel with the carnivorous beast in pursuit. We pulled him through the threshold seconds before the hungry bear slammed into the industrial strength door with an angry thud. The next day we took a tram up a mountainside. This is the precise moment I recognized my fear of heights. The fear I felt while swinging against the side of a jagged cliff left me with little appreciation for the 360° view surrounding me.

Ketchikan may have felt like an isolated rock in the middle of nowhere, but the field trips offered adventures far beyond hopping aboard a yellow school bus for a day trip to a boring museum.

Full Immersion

Ketchikan's First Lutheran Church sits high atop Tongass Avenue with a perfect steeple for eagles to perch while scanning the Tongass Narrows for an easy salmon meal. It was also a beacon for Mom and Dad. We staked our seat five rows back on the left side where Curt left his signature motorcycle drawings on the back of the pew in front of us. It wasn't long before our full immersion into the new congregation, men's club, women's group, confirmation classes for Mike, and Sunday school for Curt and me.

My favorite part of church was coffee hour after the service. The women set out a silver tea service and beautiful cookies, carefully arranged on fancy plates. The lemon bars were dreamy and the Norwegian buttery lefse melted on my tongue. A wonderful old German fellow would bring industrial-sized plastic bowls bursting with strawberry gelatin and sliced bananas, and plop them down right next to the delicate cookie plates, much to the chagrin of the proper Norwegian Ladies.

It seemed there was a new baby baptized every week and soon I would find myself enjoying goodies in congregant's living rooms while watching their children.

Shopping Shore Side

I loved the freedom of being able to walk downtown by myself to spend my babysitting money on clothes and jewelry, and there was a tiny dress shop across the street from City Float that I visited often. As the owner bent over her sewing machine creating delightful dresses, she was exceedingly patient with my chatter and zeal as I tried on all her latest creations. Swathed from head to toe in floral prints, luxurious velvets, and yards of ecru lace, it was impossible not to feel lovely.

Feminine frocks aside, one outfit stood out among all others. I'd managed to make the youth football cheerleading team and I was proud of my white sweatshirt with its blue horseshoe insignia. Mom wrangled yards of royal blue fabric rushing through her sewing machine as she constructed my short circular skirt.

As I jumped around in the mud with drenched pigtails stuck to my neck and fuzzy blue and white ribbons staining my sweatshirt, it was apparent I lacked a bit of coordination. I had no idea about the finer points of football but I could jump up and down and yell for my Colts:

Hold that line. Hit 'em hard. Make 'em fight for every yard.

Up a Creek

Though I was by myself for most of my shopping excursions downtown I always felt safe, even as I passed dozens of bars containing lively patrons. Downtown Ketchikan had a bar every few feet and I think the city may have held more liquor licenses per capita than any other community in the country during the 1970s and 1980s. Public drunkenness was commonplace, and I soon learned which characters to avoid and which old salts added local color.

Mom was doing some shopping downtown on a bitter rainy afternoon when a man stumbled out from a bar threshold and started yelling at her.

"Hey lady!" Mom picked up her pace.

"Hey lady!" Mom's stylish high-heeled boots clicked a rapid beat on the pavement but he stumbled after her and tugged on her arm. Turning to face her assailant, she hissed, "What do you want?"

"Hey lady, where'd you get them fancy boots?" She couldn't help but laugh, and this local fellow became one of our favorite Ketchikan characters, always generous with a greeting and a smile.

A couple blocks from where Mom met her admirer, a small hamlet of colorful buildings line Creek Street—the infamous boardwalk of ill repute—that is anchored by "Dolly's House" in the old Red Light District. The Shamrock Bar—*The Chapel by the Sea*—sat just around the corner on Stedman Street where a lap dance, barroom brawl, and dancers hailing the fishermen at Thomas Basin float, were as commonplace as church on Sunday. Bona fide men of the cloth, along with their congregants, ultimately stormed City Council to call for an end to the debauchery. They managed to squelch the shenanigans, but not before I bore witness to a few curbside scuffles.

Street scenes, sidewalk brawls, public drunkenness and profanity, while at times appalling, and even bloody, added color to a wet and hazy world. Sometimes we turned our heads in disgust, sometimes we found hilarity, and sometimes Mom drove the car around the block for a second look.

Chapter 4

We moved across town to Deermount Street, at the base of Deer Mountain, the summer before I enrolled in Schoenbar Junior High. Situated on the corner of Park Avenue and Bear Valley Road, the school was just a short walk from home.

By the time school started, I'd made a couple new friends who knew their way around the neighborhood. Tammie lived just around the corner on Park Avenue. Her family was jovial and noisy and their door was always open for visitors. Unlike our home, where major baking was for special occasions, it seemed every day was reason to celebrate at Tammie's. As soon as I stepped into the living room of the friendly neighborhood bakery, her flour-dusted mother would push aside baking supplies and invite me to take a seat at the Formica table. I laughed and swapped stories with the family as she pulled sticky, buttery cinnamon rolls from the oven and then set a perfect mound of heaven on my plate. Melty chocolate chip cookies and other tasty treats followed as I ate myself into sugar oblivion. After eating our fill, Tammie's dad would pull out his black guitar and sing a few tunes as Tammie joined in harmony.

Ginny lived a bit closer to town on a house up several sets of stairs that overlooked Ketchikan Creek. I often spent the night at Ginny's, where we stayed up until the wee hours giggling, listening to 45s, poring over teen magazines, and dreaming about people and places far beyond Ketchikan.

The transition between grade school and junior high tested my stamina physically, socially, and emotionally. My high-powered glasses must have magnified my eyes and, to my horror, some boys started calling me "Frog." I was already self-conscious about getting chubby, now I knew the boys thought I was ugly. Full of self-loathing, I lashed out against Mom every time she tried to comfort me. What could she possibly know about teenage angst? Either she let me ramble about my unfortunate life, or she bit back and told me to stop feeling sorry for myself. It was during one of our arguments that I told her I hated her. Dad had to spank his wayward teenager and it was so humiliating I never said those cruel words again. I was mouthy and bitchy at home and insecure and giggly in school. The solace of friends made those difficult years bearable, but self-doubts fed my insecurities, and I knew I was the most pitiful looking girl in school.

Crossing the Line

I was never leery about walking back and forth to school until I encountered the girls I'll call the Bear Valley Bullies—the meanest, toughest girls in school. The ringleader and her cronies had already shoved Tammie's head into a drinking fountain in the cafeteria. Always ready to rumble, they would attack without provocation. Cutting across the ballpark after school one day, I walked past the dugout where the bullies were hanging out smoking cigarettes. I nodded and kept walking but was suddenly ensnared by a rabid pack of bitches. The circle of girls grew tighter, the smaller girls like a wolf pack nipping at my heels, tearing at my hair, while the alpha leader bared her fangs and slowly moved in for the kill. An entire percussion section was banging in my chest. Without letting go of a single tear or giving my attackers the satisfaction of begging for mercy, I raised my hands to my face for protection, lowered my head, and prepared for my pummeling into the baseball diamond. A friend of the ringleader happened upon the battlefield. She was my former neighbor at the apartment across town and the biggest girl in school. I forced a feeble smile, and squeaked out, "Hi." She became my instant hero when she called foul on the proceedings. I sprinted across the ball field intent on a homerun to Deermount Street, not once looking back to see if the bullies were in pursuit.

I ventured onto a popular shortcut called the Schoenbar Trail one afternoon on my way to Lutheran confirmation class. A few paces into my jaunt, I spied some of my neighbors and a few Bear Valley Bullies passing a pipe. They grinned deviously and invited me to join them. I calculated the what-ifs: If I didn't join them and they were caught they would think I was a narc. If I joined them I wouldn't be able to tell, but who knew what might happen? Not sure I'd survive another encounter with the bullies, I chose the latter option. A boy held the pipe in my mouth as I sucked a chimney's worth of smoke into my lungs. It was a comical coughing session and we all laughed as smoke spewed from my nose and mouth and dissipated under dripping trees. The event was over rapidly but pot smoking guilt hung over my head. Not ready to confess my marijuana indoctrination at Lutheran confirmation, I skipped the Bible class, walked back home, and once again shared secrets with Slippers.

Craggy Shorelines

I was finally old enough for church camp, the consolation prize for sitting through hours of boring confirmation lessons. Mike always seemed to have so much fun at Lutherwood in Washington, and I had been waiting for years for the same experience: swimming and canoeing in a warm lake, arts and crafts, and meeting hundreds of kids from around the state.

Only four kids signed up for the Alaskan summer fun, two boys and another girl. The morning air was cool and foggy when we jumped in a skiff at Knudson Cove Marina, north of Ketchikan. The wind tangled my hair as black waves lapped the sides of the boat. Eagles sailed overhead, swooping down occasionally to snag a fish for breakfast dining in their gigantic nests. Other boaters waved as we motored along the coastline. When the sun finally broke through the clouds, the trees and moss on the rocky outcroppings shimmered green, as ducklings bobbed along the sparkling water below.

We unloaded the skiff at Grant Island. There were no new kids from other churches, or counselors to assign our rooms. There were no rooms. There was one big cabin with a wood cook stove and a loft. No arts and crafts. No mess hall or cooks to serve afternoon snacks. No running water. No latrine. I reluctantly conceded my city girl status to clueless camper. The pastor took the skiff back to town and left the four of us alone on our adventure for the day. We rowed along the shore in a tiny dinghy, and dropped a few lines in the water. Suddenly we had a bite—a big bite! We'd hooked into a huge prehistoric sea creature. Its brown body was long, flat and wide, its underside was milky white and both eyeballs were on the same side of its head. One of the guys clubbed the unfortunate halibut several times before it grudgingly succumbed to its fate. Instead of hotdogs dangling off sticks in the campfire—we enjoyed Alaskan bounty— wonderfully fresh and flavorful.

The shoreline and skyline blurred as we scavenged under seaweed covered rocks. Extreme low tides revealed thousands of slimy, bumpy, multi-colored sea cucumbers and orange and purple starfish as large as dinner plates. The tidal pools teemed with gumboots, china caps, sea anemones, urchins, and hermit crabs peeking out from borrowed shelters.

There was no pristine white sand beach and my tennis shoes never adhered to the slippery, yellow-brown, popweed that covered the rocks. There was no roped-off swimming area or floating dock with a water slide, and the water was freezing cold, but I finally took the plunge—my first official dip in Alaskan waters. It took several moments before I could breathe without gasping, but when my whole body was hypothermic purple—and I could no longer feel my extremities—I dogpaddled alongside my frozen friends.

We warmed up next to a fire, whittled some sticks, and roasted marshmallows while sharing ghost stories. As I screamed, giggled, and enjoyed the thrill of being terrified of the bogeyman, I was unaware of a more common threat of wild bears that may have been lurking in the woods.

Filthy fingernails, sticky with marshmallow goo, grimy clothes and alder smoke hair were proof of my first Alaskan camping adventure.

Other summer camping adventures would follow through the years, including joining forces with Lutheran kids from Petersburg, a smaller community north of Ketchikan known as "Little Norway." Our small group of six rode an Alaskan Marine Highway System ferry up the Inside Passage, finally arriving in Petersburg several hours later. After my previous camping experience, I should have learned a thing or two about Alaskan-style outings, but I just knew the folks in Petersburg would be sophisticated in the ways of church camp, and that the pristine lake of my dreams was about to become reality.

I bedded down on the cold floor of the church basement, stretched out in my flannel sleeping bag alongside my camp comrades, eagerly anticipating archery, waterskiing, and canoeing lessons.

Sideways rain blew me down a steep and slippery wooden ramp the next morning as I tried to ignore the skiff moored at the float. The harbor smelled like low tide and raindrops cast deep rings alongside the boat. We bobbed along the shoreline for what seemed like hours until we came to our destination.

As my comrades began their trek through the mud, wearing raingear, waterproof backpacks, and Ketchikan Tennie Runners—good ol' brown neoprene boots—I climbed out of the miserable skiff, hair matted to my head, and rain dripping down my neck, as green as the day I disembarked the Wickersham. With suitcase and purse in hand, I slogged through miles of muskeg that threatened to steal my white canvas tennis shoes, as the counselors no doubt clucked about the Cheechako in their midst. My shoes never dried out, and my clothes were moldy-damp, but burnt marshmallow s'mores, and singing Kumbaya around the campfire warmed me up enough to enjoy stories of the Kushtaka and other Alaskan lore.

Years later, I successfully talked our pastor and two confirmation classmates into attending Lutherwood. I couldn't wait to jump off the plane in SeaTac and head north toward a proper church camp. I attended the weeklong, orchestrated, camp and enjoyed a schoolgirl crush on a camp counselor, but I was plagued by terrible stomach pains and much of my stay was at the nurses' station. My memories of organized play at Lutherwood are dim compared to the colorful and more rugged events in Alaska.

Water Ballet

Unqualified for Alaskan adventures, I remembered football cheerleading had been fun. Even though it was cold and I wasn't the best in the league, it was hard to gauge anyone's ability as they did high kicks and cartwheels in the mud. When school started again, rather than kick up dirt clods in the ball field, I decided to try the indoor sport of ballet. I'd been in a class years before on Whidbey Island and the glitzy costumes and parasols had been great props for camouflaging my mediocre moves.

Ketchikan's ballet school was upstairs above Nordby's Marine Supply Store, which hovered over Tongass Narrows on stout wooden pilings. Serious dancing took place above the store as serious fishermen geared up for fish openings. Rugged, bearded, men, clad in boots and halibut jackets purchased lead line, twine, and floats, alongside pony-tailed ballerinas who bought Capezio slippers, pink tights, and leotards. The sweet perfumes mingled with fish aromas and creosote created a confusing olfactory sensation.

I should have skipped down the stairs and out the door after my debut on the dance floor. Slipping my small feet into shiny pink Capezios while the other girls donned scuffed slippers, or tattered toe shoes, was my first clue. I shuffled onto the floor like a St. Bernard puppy amongst sleek Greyhounds. Seasoned dancers with willowy arms and legs seemed to take flight as they glided across the floor, while I barely mastered first position. My reflection at the bar confirmed chubby and klutzy looked out of place alongside long and lithe ballerinas.

Lessons increased to several times a week in preparation for the Cinderella program. Young men from high school volunteered to escort the junior dancers in our ballroom scene. I stepped on feet. I giggled nervously. Practiced plié's or gliding glissades were forgotten skills, adding a partner—beyond comprehension.

Mom bought yards of chewed bubblegum-pink satin netting, sequins, and feathers. She hired a seamstress to make my precious finery. I spent hours standing perfectly still atop a round ottoman, being stuck by stickpins, while my measurements were carefully recorded. Finally, after what seemed like weeks, my precious costume was ready for dress rehearsal at the high school.

Veteran dance mothers rushed excited ballerinas to spare classrooms where they transformed us with cake makeup, rouge, bright-red lipstick, hairspray and spit. All rings, watches and earrings were confiscated—nothing was to detract from the beautiful set, costumes, dancers, and movement.

The seasoned dancers appeared on stage for inspection first—transformed, stunning, possessing grace and elegance that someday I would surely attain. Next came the little dancers—the darling children, whose very presence garnered oohs and aahs from the audience.

At last, it was time for the intermediate class to take the stage. The seamstress had spent hours on my dress and the cool rustling fabric felt lovely as I demurely walked across the stage—straight back, extended neck.

As our instructor inspected each girl from head to toe, checking for jewelry, loose threads, dirty slippers, I held my breath and posed in my finest ballerina position, toes pointed out and hand overhead, awaiting the highest praise. I gasped when she pulled the fabric away from my waist to emphasize I was drowning in pink satin.

Someone exclaimed, "The ugly duckling has appeared!"

The stage erupted with gasps from the mothers, giggles from the girls, and guffaws from the male escorts.

I scanned the crowd for a friendly face. My mother looked like she was going to cry.

My instructor said, "Take off those glasses."

"But I can't see without my glasses."

"You can't wear them. They will reflect the lights. Absolutely not."

I waddled off the stage.

After standing still for Mom's last minute nips and tucks, I sought solace with my friendly black Slippers wishing he'd chew up my pink ballet slippers.

The next morning I appeared on stage in my tacked and basted ugly duckling dress for my final blind curtain call.

Return to Sick Bay

Even though frogs are cute and ducklings are darling, I was not flattered by my new nicknames. I spent hours in front of my makeup mirror that had lighting for every possible occasion. I liked indoor light best, but studied myself under simulated sunlight prepared to abolish any blemish that might invite unwanted scrutiny. One morning while checking for flaws, I noticed an odd feeling bump that rolled like a marble under the skin in front of my left ear. Mom was rushing to get ready for work when I followed her into the bathroom and said, "Feel this bump." She sighed in exasperation and set down her curling iron. "What bump?"

"This one in front of my ear."

Mom shook her head. "It's probably just a swollen gland. Quit messing with it."

My scrutiny increased and I interrupted Mom's morning routine a few weeks later, insisting she feel the bump. It seemed bigger. She did a cursory check and again told me to leave it alone.

Summer turned to fall and I was busy with eighth grade activities as the steely-sized bump grew to the size and consistency of a boulder marble. I decided to pester Mom once more. This time, realizing the bump was significantly larger, she hastily made an appointment with my doctor. The doctor palpated the growth by my ear and informed my mother I had a tumor. He recommended immediate surgery.

No one told me there was a possibility the tumor was malignant or the risk of the doctor severing a nerve, which could have left me with a disfigured and partially paralyzed face. I checked into the hospital, stowed my belongings, and donned a shapeless hospital gown. A nurse came to my bedside and injected me with something to help me relax. My room suddenly felt like a walk-in freezer. Mom wrapped me in soft bleached-white blankets from the blanket warmer oven as my teeth chattered uncontrollably. Nurses pushed my gurney through ominous operating room doors where several blue-clad men and women with paper bonnets on their heads tried to find me under the blanket mounds. Soft music played in the background and staff whispered encouraging words as I descended into deep sleep.

I woke entangled in tubes, and my stomach threatened to add a bit more color to the nauseating orange walls. A dozen red roses cheered the room but their strong scent assaulted my sinuses. When I placed a finger under my nose to deter a sneeze, the IV tubing caught a sticky drainage tube clinging to the side of my neck. I was horrified when I yanked it loose, staining the turban that dwarfed my swollen face. With my enlarged head and round eyeglasses it appeared I'd been transformed into an alien.

My window offered a million dollar a view of the waterfront activity. Floatplanes buzzed by as nurses flitted in and out of my room. Mom was a constant companion as she read *All Creatures Great and Small* to me; and instead of singing in the church choir on Easter Sunday, she spent the day at my bedside—no doubt praising God that her child too had dislodged the stone.

I did not have cancer or a paralyzed face. Except for a small bit of numbness, and the fact that my cheek turns bright red when I eat something tart, my face healed and went right back to its normal condition. A faint scar from the top of my ear to my jaw line is the only remnant of my weeklong hospital stay.

Bon Voyage

After my forced convalescence, I was glad to be back to my normal routine. I patted Slippers on the head and tickled him behind the ears before leaving for school. I was pretending interest in a science experiment when the school nurse summoned me to her office and gently closed the door of the antiseptic room. She sat next to me and took my small hand in her veiny one. The room was stifling and her clammy skin hinted that something terrible had happened.

The nurse uttered words impossible to fathom. "Your mother called and asked me to have you wait for her here. I'm so sorry. Your dog has died."

I started screaming and sobbing. Slippers, my faithful companion, my best friend, the silver lining to that ridiculous easy bake sewing machine mix up, and the one that crawled under the covers with me every night, couldn't possibly be dead.

I escaped the nurse's office and ran home to find Morgan, our black lab, howling and pawing at the sliding glass door. Dad had placed my sweet black Cockapoo on the kitchen throw rug in front of the sink before he left, allowing me time to say goodbye. Slippers didn't look dead. I curled up next to him, stroked his soft curls and begged him to wake up. Dad came home and joined me on the floor. Tears saturated Slipper's coat as Morgan continued his mournful death howl outside. I sobbed myself to sleep every night for weeks and was sure I would never recover.

After spending days in the hospital, showing up in school with bandages on my neck, and the loss of my beloved Slippers, all my previous sorrows and problems seemed trivial.

Chapter 5

I was happy to be done with junior high and eager to begin high school. I'd been busy babysitting neighborhood kids all summer and earned enough for my first flight south by myself to buy a new wardrobe. My Aunt Jean and cousin Lorri picked me up at SeaTac and introduced me to the Tacoma Mall. Window displays of beautiful clothes enticed me into boutique shops, and girls at the makeup counters doused me in fruity perfumes and transformed my pale skin into a rosy glow. Finally satisfied I had enough clothes and makeup for the school year, I twirled and posed in front of Lorri and her sister, Karen as they patiently indulged my excitement. This was so much better than ordering hope-for-the-best clothing from the catalog, waiting weeks for them to arrive on the slow boat, only to find they didn't fit, or worse, to wear an outfit to school on the same day as a beautiful skinny minny.

I was enjoying a fashionable high school freshman debut at Kayhi, giggling with girlfriends, flirting with boys, and trying to take my studies seriously, but every couple of weeks I woke up feeling as if someone was kicking me in the stomach with steel-toed boots. It was painfully exhausting for the whole family as I retched for hours into bowls that Dad emptied all night long. My stomach would be so sore the following morning the thought of wearing constricting clothes was unbearable.

The episodes became more frequent, the kicks to my gut more intense. It was difficult to concentrate at school when I felt sick so often. After a particularly violent episode Mom managed to get me a morning appointment with the same doctor who removed my tumor. She described my ailment to the nurse who scribbled on her clipboard until the doctor came in and asked a few more questions. The doc hemmed and hawed knowingly before he left the room. The nurse came back with a silver tray holding a strange looking instrument. She handed me a gown and small towel, told me to take off my undies, and left before hearing my protests.

Mom looked concerned as my confusion became apparent. Whatever was about to happen, I didn't want her there, but I was reluctant to have her leave. The nurse came back in and had me lay back while she pulled out a pair of mechanical covered horseshoes from each side of the examining table. She asked me to place my feet in the tube sock covered contraptions. I was nearly upside down at this point and feeling completely vulnerable.

Curiously, someone had taped a poster to the ceiling. I stared at it while hoping for a cosmic event to knock me off the table. The doctor came back in and nodded at Mom. She stood next to the table and took my hand. The nurse patted my other hand and once again told me to relax.

Seconds later I felt the speculum inside as the doctor gently pushed on my tummy from the outside. It felt like he had skewered me with a red-hot poker. The sterile room had morphed into a torture chamber. While I recovered from that event, I learned about another as the doctor wrote orders for emergency surgery.

Once settled at the hospital, a starched white nurse came to my bedside and poked me in the hip with the longest needle I'd ever seen. Whatever was in the needle parched my throat and it felt like I'd swallowed a bag of cotton balls. I asked for water, but the hospital strictly enforced its prohibition on food or drink before surgery. I couldn't even suck on ice chips. A merciful nurse finally conceded a damp washcloth. I curled up in the fetal position and pitifully sucked moisture from the rag.

As my parents bid me farewell at the double doors, I entrusted them with my glasses, the equivalent of handing over my eyeballs, which created an unusual scene:

Green aliens with fuzzy blue bonnets wheeled me into the operating room as hazy faces floated above me. Intermittent beeps, whirs and rock music set the tone for my second trip to outer space. A humongous flying saucer hovered directly above my head as the aliens asked me to count backwards, 100, 99, 98, 97, 96 ...

While I slumbered, the doctor inserted a laparoscope into my belly button and diagnosed the disaster. A pinhole in my appendix had been leaking toxins into my abdomen and like a tire that eventually pops, my appendix finally burst.

I woke up to a nurse hovering over me and instantly decided I needed to go back to sleep. "How's the pain?" I attempted to focus my blind eyes on her, and give her the *duh* look, right before I threw up all over myself. She cupped an emesis basin under my chin. In two nauseous waves, an ocean's worth of bile overflowed the basin and sullied her uniform.

My stomach burned under mounds of bandages and adhesive tape and even though I felt I'd severely compromised the green team's work—the six-inch seam held. Shortly after the vomiting incident, and while I was barely coherent, the nurse came back in and tried to coax me into walking.

It is nearly impossible to walk with a gaping hole in your side, but I smiled weakly and tried to make up for the earlier projectile assault. The world spun when I tried to stand, and my blood pressure dropped just enough to buy me more time to recover.

It was a sweaty and grimy ordeal and I was desperate to have my hair washed. After I offered much whining and pleading, a nurse secured a weird contraption around my head—kind of like the cones they put around dogs to keep them from chewing their bandages off—and the suds and water drained into a big plastic tub right there in bed.

I spent several days in the hospital and was finally able to go home, where I spent days peeling adhesive tape off my tummy.

Doldrums

Now that I'd recovered from two major surgeries I should have been feeling rejuvenated, but it seemed I was puttering along on fumes. My folks never seemed particularly concerned about my grades and I was a champion procrastinator. I greeted dawn on countless occasions as I tried to write last-minute essays, adding to my continued fatigue. Rather than impress my teachers with study habits and good grades, I chose to bribe them for extra time by baking them chocolate chip cookies. Though I wasn't pressured to make perfect grades, I always had to have a job, which kept me busy and disconnected from after school clubs or activities. I was out the door and off to work as soon as the bell rang.

About once a year, I'd be hit by a virus that had me wandering the maroon corridors of Kayhi at the speed of a sloth. It was all I could do to carry my books from one class to the other. My throat burned, food scalded my tongue, and my stomach hurt. All I wanted to do was curl up under a desk with a blankie. I had symptoms of mono, yet the tests came back negative. With no diagnosis, there was no cure and the only remedy was to relax and sleep it off—the perfect excuse for my chronic procrastination.

There was no better prescription than giggling with my girlfriends at slumber parties and no better distraction than heartbreaking romances with boyfriends. Still, a nagging stomachache festered and the fierce grip of fatigue zapped my energy.

Drowning In My Tears

The rainy summer days in Ketchikan brightened considerably when the seine fleet showed up for the commercial salmon-fishing season. Nothing woke me up faster than the arrival of boatloads of tanned young men from the Lower 48, eager to catch fish, earn cash, and snag a summertime girlfriend. I was as pale as a halibut and was enthralled by exotic sun-kissed fishermen who looked like sun gods. One evening a purse seine crew sat behind my girlfriends and me at the Coliseum Theater. Their ongoing banter distracted us from what was happening onscreen. No longer interested in the movie, we joined the conversation and offered them a ride back to Bar Harbor for the beginning of our summer fun. Giggling teenage girls, hanging out at a marina full of tanned and transient fishermen: what could be better?

We scurried over boats tied five deep in the harbor and met many partying crews of bearded fishermen as we climbed from deck to deck. Our new friends worked on a lovely wooden boat and they gave us a tour of their summer home. There were a couple bunks topside for the captain and the cook. The rest of the crew bunked next to the noisy engine room in the claustrophobic foc'sle, which reeked of a bilge mixture of fish gurry, diesel, saltwater and sweat. After the tour, I climbed out of the foc'sle eager for fresh air.

Seine net and corks were piled high on deck and the block hung precariously overhead. The deck had an appealing aroma of Old Spice, barbecued salmon, and coffee, which blended with the smells of the harbor. I glommed on to the cook and planted myself at the galley table to sample his creations, or on the seine skiff perched on the stern if the weather supported a barbecue.

My summer revolved around fish closures, almost qualifying me a true Alaskan, except I didn't have a clue about the Alaskan fishery, just the men catching the fish. I spent many evenings standing at the top of Bar Harbor Marina, or out on the breakwater anxiously awaiting a seine boat on the horizon. There was no set schedule and the wait was frustrating. Such was life for a fisherman's girl.

The end of my summer romance happened abruptly on my birthday. On August 7, I got the word. The crew was stowing gear, battening down hatches, and preparing to toss the lines. This was so unexpected! I didn't appreciate the fickle fishing season. I'd expected three more weeks of fun to lead me into the school year. I walked about two miles from my house to the fuel dock to find out the truth for myself. My fisherman walked me back home under a moonlit sky, tucked a plucked "he loves me" daisy behind my ear, and carried me —honeymoon style—through Ketchikan's Grassy Park. He kissed me goodbye on the front porch and vowed to write regularly.

An empty mailbox taunted me every day and I thought I'd die before I received a letter about two weeks later. It was time for my annual school-clothes shopping extravaganza in Seattle. I invited my two girlfriends to come along, and since we were visiting my cousin Lorri in Bremerton, we planned a rendezvous with the crew, just a short ferry ride across Puget Sound. We spent an anxious morning curling our hair, picking out outfits and chattering about seeing our fishermen again. Unfortunately, just before we left for the ferry we learned only one of the crew would be able to meet us and it wasn't the one I wanted to see. My eagerly anticipated reunion had been shanghaied.

I'd planned on starting my junior year with whopper-sized stories about my summer fling. By mid-September I was so depressed I lost all interest in school. Undeterred by the disastrous reunion, my girlfriend Aleta and I planned another trip to Seattle to meet with the guys.

We met them at Seattle Center. Aleta and her beau did not contain their zeal as they wandered off to enjoy the day, but I detected a chilly tone in my fisherman's voice that matched the coldness of the frozen raspberry yogurt cone he dropped on my white pants. He did not apologize and he seemed genuinely miserable to be with me. After about twenty minutes, he made up an excuse to leave and left me at the fountain, utterly alone, amongst the crowd. My carefully chosen white pants were stained fuchsia, matching the blotchiness of my tear-stung cheeks. I'd wasted my summer earnings just to have someone stomp on my heart. I took my seat on the plane, next to happy Aleta, and flew back home wondering why my summer romance had sunk into the cold dark sea.

No Wind in My Sails

If I was fatigued before, I was thoroughly exhausted by my senior year, especially in concert band class. The classical music lulled me into la la land and all I wanted to do was sleep. Practicing my clarinet was not high on my list of priorities, and my lack of effort did not make me a valued band member. I'd joined band in fifth grade but never made significant progress. Practicing at home was an unpopular pastime and Morgan howled pitifully as I practiced scales. Even the dog had better tone than I did.

Year after year, I warmed the last chair of the clarinet section as underclassmen moved up the ranks. Concert band was right before lunch and I was always impossibly tired at that time of day. While other kids performed beautiful melodies, I stifled yawns, held my distended tummy, and fidgeted in my chair. When my teacher invited me to hang up my horn, I explained to him quitting was not acceptable to my parents. I wasted both my time and his as I squeaked out tunes all through high school. The absolute worst part about being a terrible clarinet player was proving I deserved last chair. Sitting alone in the tiny windowed tryout room with the ominous recording machine, I kept waiting for an opportunity to play without an audience on the other side of the pane. When no opportunity came, I finally pressed the big red button. What I lacked in musicality I made up for in a brilliant staccato of expletives catalogued on cassette tapes for eternity.

The End of the Line

I was anxious to bid Kayhi farewell by the end of my senior year. I was also eager to escape the gauntlet of jeering boys who dramatically fell against their lockers if an overweight girl walked by and who still called me *Frog* every day as I walked past "Stud Corner." Even though I had a boyfriend in school now, I wasn't immune to the name calling. One day one of the culprits crept up behind me and repeatedly yelled *Frog* in my ear while I was trying to talk with my science teacher. I could feel my fist ball up. I paused my studious conversation with my science teacher, turned around, and slugged the loudmouth in the face. One stud down and the victory was delicious.

Hanging out after school one day during a rare respite from work, I encountered a group of four underclassmen boys who made the moniker of Frog seem tame by comparison. I was meeting my girlfriend in a classroom when I heard them taunting her with sexually explicit names and threats. I had never experienced such blatant misogyny and couldn't believe what they were saying. My friend was doing her best to ignore them, but they wouldn't shut up. I grabbed a lock of the ringleader's hair and yanked hard.

"Get your fucking hand off me, bitch."

The more he yelled the harder I pulled. His cronies threatened me and told me to let go but I had so much adrenaline in my fingertips they seemed glued to his head. I pulled even harder and dared them to say another word. A teacher finally arrived and convinced me to let go.

The next day I was called to the principal's office for the humiliating task of reciting word-for-word the things I'd heard the day before. I didn't have to apologize and the foul-mouthed thugs got kicked out of school for a few days. Words hurt. Defending myself against them was preparing me to fight much more sinister ones in a few years.

When the day finally came to graduate, my glasses reflected the stage lights as I floated across the Cinderella stage of my ballet days and gracefully accepted my diploma.

I had no particular goal for life after high school, but my graduation present of oversized Dijon mustard colored luggage was a strong hint I needed a plan. No school counselors had spoken with me about opportunities beyond the walls of Kayhi, but a college recruiter from a small Christian college in Issaquah, WA came to our church and spoke with some of the kids. I thought it sounded like a good ticket off the rock, so I signed on and looked forward to moving to civilization at the end of the summer.

Fickle Winds

The summer before I left for college I got a job at a brand new ice cream shop downtown, directly across from the cruise ship dock. On opening day, thousands of senior citizens needing a snack after their wild Alaskan experience moved in hungrily. Mobs of locals, loggers, and fishermen joined the tourists on the other side of the cooler. There amongst the mass of anxious faces was the smiling captain from the seine boat of my past summer fun. He told me most of the crew had returned and promised to tell them hello for me.

After a particularly stressful day in Ice Cream Land, my boyfriend of the last few months broke up with me. I wasn't happy about it, but it wasn't entirely unexpected. Fortunately, I met a new boy in the neighborhood named Grant who was working at a local fish cannery with Curt. In between days of gutting fish on the cannery slime line, they massacred entire countries in the game of RISK. I couldn't have asked for a better salve for the breakup than a 6'2" young man with long dark hair, and amazing blue-gray eyes, sprawled out in the living room.

A few evenings after the breakup, I was lurking over the RISK board when I got a call the fisherman who'd left me crying by the fountain in Seattle. He asked if I had time to see him that evening. Eager to hear why he'd left me, I accepted his invitation. This should prove to cannery boy what a catch I was.

I chose a flattering outfit and was eager to show my fisher friend I was no longer the young seine boat groupie who would giggle at everything he said. A more sophisticated me greeted him at the top of Ryus Float and drove him to Bugge Beach, a few miles south of town. It was a beautiful evening, perfect for a walk along the water. We found a nice warm rock to sit on, and after exchanging trivial niceties, he apologized for treating me so badly in Seattle. He was truly sorry. I accepted his apology, eager to salvage our sunken romance and breathe some life into my summer. He was so happy about my graciousness he invited me to his upcoming wedding. Ugh. I'd left the game of RISK and took a detour through the game of SORRY.

Much to my delight, the neighbors who were hosting the neighbor boy invited our family to spend a weekend with them at a forest service cabin at Helm Bay. The seas were calm when we left Clover Pass Marina, and I was excited about spending a weekend with my good-looking new friend. The cabin was well equipped with built-in bunks, and the old-growth Sitka Spruce and Western Hemlock offered shelter as we camped in the middle of the rainforest. A slight drizzle kept us hydrated and our two families enjoyed barbecued hamburgers, salmon, and the few wild blueberries left the bears hadn't pawed through. The boat ride over had been calm and there were no problems anticipated for the return trip to Clover Pass.

Williwaw
(A sudden violent wind)

On the day of our return to Clover Pass Marina, the winds whipped up a Williwaw. We ran out of fuel and bobbed helplessly as huge swells lapped at the sides of our boat. Spare jugs of fuel mocked Dad as he went tharn. I hadn't been overly frightened of the water, but that experience—seeing the fear in Dad's eyes—well, I started humming hymns—*Jesus Loves Me, Amazing Grace*—as the death knell kept time in my ears. We were in safer waters when I emerged from hiding under the boat cushions in the bow. Misty rain-filtered sun danced on the water, Dall Porpoise leaped playfully next to the boat, but I had no appreciation for their beauty. When the captain panicked, he awakened a fear in me that dampened any enjoyment for Alaskan adventures for years. Each time an opportunity for boating arose, I found multiple excuses to stay off the water. I never regained my sea legs, relegating myself to a self-imposed Alaskatraz prison on Revillagigedo Island.

The camping trip solidified my relationship with the boy next door and he and I spent a fun summer enjoying walks at Ward Lake and Settlers Cove. When we decided to hike up Deer Mountain we asked Curt to come along. Right after vamping for photos on a small pack of snow, Curt and Grant went off trail and left me alone on the mountaintop. I was so furious I ran all the way down the mountain and probably could have outrun a black bear if I'd run into one on the trail.

Grant made up for ditching me on the mountainside by buying me dinner and champagne at a fancy restaurant for my nineteenth birthday. The champagne was so expensive he had no money left for a tip, and neither one of us had considered he was still a minor. He paid the check and we scooted on out of the restaurant before anyone noticed our transgressions.

Fish Out of Water

After scooping ice cream all summer, I was ready to trade an aching wrist for writer's cramp and begin my college adventure. I packed my entire wardrobe into my yellow suitcases, waved goodbye to my family and flew to Seattle. When I stepped into my dorm room, my luggage engulfed about 1/3 of the space. The remote campus, situated in the hills above Issaquah, WA, had previously been a convent. The closets were large enough to hold a nun habit and little else. I stuffed as much as I could into the cubicle, shoved the rest under my bed, and placed my radio on the windowsill eager to find out how many stations were available.

After a few weeks in my new home, it was evident I was out of place. Someone commented on my choice of "secular music," as if it was a sin, and though she didn't speak for the majority, it caused me to question my motivations for being there in the first place. I was accustomed to the spirited lingo from my rough and tumble town and I'd dialed in some great rock music which I preferred to spiritual meditations and praise anthems. My RISK playing boyfriend had moved back to Washington and he often picked me up to spend the weekend with his family in Kelso, Washington. Grant would step out of his Oldsmobile Cutlass reeking of pot, while the fellows on campus sported wholesome milk moustaches.

Chapel services took place mid-morning, but my attendance was dismal. My stomach problems were getting worse and my abdomen would swell after every meal. Instead of kneeling in prayer in the sanctuary, I'd lie prostrate in my bed praying for my stomach to stop hurting. As I snoozed, my friends enjoyed all kinds of activities. My grandparents also lived in Kelso, and when Grant couldn't pick me up, I often took the bus to spend quiet evenings at their house and sleep as much as possible

I decided not to return to college for a second year. I wasn't a serious student and I was conflicted by attention from mid-western, Bible-toting students and my rebellious pot-smoking boyfriend. I was almost twenty years old, I never felt good, and I had no direction in my life.

Chapter 6

I worked the summer at Ketchikan Visitor's Bureau and decided to rent an apartment with my new friend and co-worker Nancy. The visitor's bureau was on the dock where crazily clad tourists clamored for first place in line for tour buses or bathrooms. We greeted thousands of folks who were eager to learn more about the town we took for granted. Sure, they asked ridiculous questions, like "How high above sea level are you?" or "Do you take American money?" but they were a happy bunch and I loved telling them about Ketchikan. I stifled my giggles, pointed out the boat they had just disembarked, showed them highlights on the walking tour map, and assured them the merchants would gladly accept their US currency. Many of the tourists, especially the men, wanted to experience the livelier side of Ketchikan. Rather than piling onto a bus with a hundred other folks they wanted downtown—no shopping, no trinkets—they wanted good old Alaskan-sized stories to take home to their buddies. With proper questioning, we ascertained the type of adventure they were hoping to find. Perhaps the Sourdough Bar to check out the photographic history of early Ketchikan, or a rowdier bar where they might witness a barroom brawl or two? Maybe they'd like The Frontier Bar where they could take part in the melodrama *The Fish Pirate's Daughter,* or for the truly adventurous . . .The Shamrock with its brazen dancers, just around the corner from Dolly's House.

I had the task of leading guided tours through Dolly's house where wisecracking duffers asked if I was Dolly, and propositioned me on a daily basis.

Grant was back for the summer and working at the cannery. I loved it when he stopped by my work or took me out to lunch for fresh halibut and fries on the dock. When his visits declined in frequency, it became apparent he preferred getting stoned to spending time with his girlfriend, a mellow experience for which I could not compete. By mid-summer we made the painful decision to call it quits, though I remained friends with him and his family for years.

It was during my stint on the dock that Nancy introduced me to a redheaded, pipe-smoking leprechaun, named Mike. He grew up in Ketchikan but was a few years older, so we had not been in school together. He had a twinkle in his eye and a wry sense of humor. He didn't seem particularly interested in me—I'm not sure he even liked me—which challenged me to have him take notice. His standoffish, couldn't-care-less attitude was entirely frustrating and I proceeded on a singular mission to win his heart.

Making Waves

My summer job ended when the last straggling tourists waved goodbye from the massive cruise ships and floated back down south. Jobs were plentiful and I found a new one in the kitchen at the hospital in Ketchikan. The chief bottle washers and experienced cooks did not appreciate a new girl in the kitchen. I walked the pots and pans gauntlet every morning and was relegated to a different table during break time as they dished about their antics from the night before. They laughed and smoked and cussed and flirted with the early-bird surgery crew as I sat alone. It wasn't until I joined them at the Totem Bar and showed them I knew a few cusswords too that I was invited to the cook's table.

My apartment was a mile or so above the hospital and Nancy and I enjoyed easy access to our jobs. When my alarm clock chimed at 04:30 a.m., I could roll out of bed and roll into work within minutes. Nancy worked swing shift in another department of the hospital so we crossed paths coming and going to work.

I would often wait for Nancy's shift to end and then she and I would head downtown where the party was just getting started. We wandered up and down the hill between the Frontier Bar and the Fireside Lounge into the wee hours of the morning, accepting free drinks from hopeful young men along the way.

While Nancy and I were out carousing, Mike was content taking long draws of sweet tobacco, and watching movies for hours on end at home. He didn't seem to mind my company, but was in no hurry to take me anywhere. He lived at his folks' house, high atop Deermount Street, while they resided in a logging camp. Typical of a number of homes in Ketchikan, there was no road access to the house. The only way to get there was to climb up about a zillion steps. By the time I made it to the front door I felt like I'd summited Deer Mountain. For some inexplicable reason I hoofed it up those steps for over a year trying to convince Mike I was special, but our relationship remained undefined. He just rocked contentedly in an overstuffed easy chair, smoked his pipe, and chuckled at me while I tried to catch my breath after my long climb.

Setting a Course for Seattle

Mike's standoffishness and his pipe tobacco had an inexplicable catnip effect on me. I was sure he cared for me; we'd been in our unconventional relationship for over a year, but I missed hanging out with friends and get-togethers—a reality that seemed impossible to enjoy with him. Eventually I grew weary of our stagnant relationship and decided to reevaluate my future.

Tracy, my best friend from college, suggested I move to Seattle. The city sounded good to me and within days, I quit my job, said my goodbyes, and lugged my yellow suitcases onto the airport ferry.

We lived in a stately old home right above The Ave. in the U-District. The bedrooms were huge with beautiful crown molding and wood flooring. I bought myself a peach and cream-colored bedroom set and basked in the loftiness of my new throw pillows. I had filled the belly of the plane with all of my belongings, and I was ever so happy to see that my room had a walk-in closet.

While Tracy worked on her Master's Degree in psychology, I spent my days trying to navigate the city. Unlike Ketchikan, no friends drove by and turned around to pick me up when I waved, so I quickly learned the bus schedules. As Tracy drove to school each day, I set out on foot, desperate to find work. I hadn't considered the difficulty of finding a job in the U-District in the summer. The competition was alarming: starving University of Washington student trying to further their college education, or aimless Ketchikanite on sabbatical from her inattentive boyfriend.

I spent my days filling out applications, playing tourist, sunbathing at Green Lake, and waiting for Tracy to quit studying. I never did find a job, but I got to know the U-District fairly well. I loved to take the bus to Pike Place Market to look at all the colorful wares and laugh as tourists got excited about vendors tossing fish, or hit Nordstroms for a day of power shopping. I also met some of the local shopkeepers and staff. One young man at a shop on The Ave. took a liking to me and I ran into him often on my walks. He gave me his number and offered to walk me home one afternoon, but I'd politely declined.

I was home alone on a Saturday evening eating a bagel and watching TV when I heard a loud thud at the living room window just inches away. My teeth clenched around the chewy dough while my feet refused to budge. Glued to the sofa, I pondered my options. I gingerly reached beside me and doused the light then crouched down and duck-walked to the TV to turn it off. There was more racket at the window as someone tried to jimmy the lock. I drew my knees to my chest and huddled on the floor.

I was alone, terrified, and hobbled by fear. I could have heard a spider crawling in the basement. I was sure my assailant could hear the bass drum in my heart between the few feet separating us. I willed myself to breathe, to get to the phone, to call for help. I knew whoever was there, knew that someone had been in the living room watching TV.

Somehow, my cement-laden body crawled to the end table, where I gently pulled the phone to the floor and quickly dialed the police. It didn't take long for my heroes in blue to show up. They checked the perimeter and then came in and made sure there was no stranger hiding upstairs under the beds, or in a secret tunnel in the basement. After they secured the house, I offered them some coffee, a place to sit in the living room, and tried to expend some nervous energy.

"What is your name?"

"Rebecca Holman."

"Do you go by Becky?"

"Sometimes, it depends."

"Rebecca, how long have you lived here?"

I smiled at the cute officer. "Oh about a month or so."

"Do you have any enemies?"

"Well, there was that one person in…"

The officer smiled patiently, "Do you have any enemies here?"

I took a sip of coffee. "No."

"What about a boyfriend, any fighting with your boyfriend?"

Finally, someone wanted to know about Mike. "Well I wouldn't really call it fighting—but it is why I moved here."

The officer raised his eyebrows and started taking notes. "Tell me more about your boyfriend."

"Oh he lives in Ketchikan…I moved down here to decide if we should stay together."

The officer looked sideways at me. "Where'd you say you moved from?"

I smiled again. "Ketchikan."

"Can you please spell that?" The officer looked at his companion who shrugged his shoulders and shook his head.

"K-E-T-C-H-I-K-A-N"

In Alaska?

"Yes."

"Rebecca, have you talked with your boyfriend recently?"

"Yes."

My hero was beginning to look exasperated. "When?"

"About an hour ago, he called from Ketchikan right before I heard the noise outside the window."

I can't be sure, but I think the officer may have run a line through the last set of notes before starting a new line of questioning.

"Okay, Rebecca, let's go back to earlier today. Did you go anywhere?"

I stood up, peered out the window.

"Rebecca, please step away from the window."

I told him about my day: walked down to The Ave. grabbed lunch at the Unicorn, picked up some pictures and talked to the kid I always run into down there.

"Tell me about the kid you talked to."

"He's kind of cute, really sweet. I talk to him all the time. He asked for my number last week, and offered to walk me home when I ran into him by the bookstore today, but I said no."

The office looked at his partner who said, "Tell me what he looked like."

"He's tall and slender, dark eyes."

"Do you know his name?"

"Yes."

After I told them his name, the officers sat me back down on the couch and explained to me that they weren't sure if this kid was the same one they were thinking of, but if so, he was a well-known popcorn pimp.

"A what?"

The officer explained a popcorn-pimp is a young recruit for the bigger pimps. One they can arrest, but whose penalties are far less severe as a juvenile than that of older pimps. He was probably hanging out at the store, but not working there except as a recruiter.

Pimps? Popcorn? What the heck? I felt like a modern-day Dorothy, befuddled in the Land of Oz. I have no idea if the attempted break-in was a random act from a bumbling burglar, or if I'd foiled the Jiffy Pop Man. And I didn't stick around to find out.

I missed Mike. He'd sent me a letter telling me how much he missed me, renewing my hope that our relationship had merit. My roommate was a serious student too busy to entertain her dependent friend. I'd depleted most of my savings, and I was tired of playing tourist at Pike Place. I wanted to enjoy life on the shore and eat some salmon in a quiet town without the crowds.

I packed up my roomful of belongings, bid Tracy adieu, and buckled myself into a plane headed for home, only to arrive there to find Mike was gone. He had been in Seattle for a week before I moved back, and had not attempted to call me. I couldn't understand how he could have been in Seattle, while I was fighting off popcorn-pimps, and not even have called.

Coming About

Not only had I done a U-turn on Alaska Airlines, I jumped right back in to my relationship with Mike and moved about 100 paces down the hall to my new job in Central Supply at the hospital. Nancy worked night shift there and seemed to enjoy the work. I began working the day shift, and it was an interesting job. I learned how to put together surgical and OB trays and was responsible for sterilizing and memorizing all of the surgical instruments, unwittingly assembling trays with the very tools that would eventually cut into me.

It was during my hospital employment stint that I really started feeling ill. My stomach hurt constantly. To make matters more difficult, the hazing in Central Supply seemed worse than in the kitchen. I was the fresh-faced new girl with a steady boyfriend with no reason to complain. A co-worker overheard other employees gossiping—that I was faking my symptoms so I could sneak to the bathroom to smoke cigarettes. In reality, I was "sneaking" to the bathroom lounge to lie down on the filthy beige vinyl couch to try to get some relief.

I visited the ER or clinic a number of times because of unbearable pain. It was always the same routine. I would be tested for a urinary tract infection, given the requisite pelvic exam, and be sent on my way with antibiotics, which were destined to fail. I was on a fruitless quest to find out what was ailing me. I was certain everyone thought I was a delusional attention whore creating an illness for kicks.

While I was still working in Central Supply, the traveling urologist came to town. I scheduled an appointment, had an exam, and before I knew it I was scheduled for a cystoscopy. It was supposed to be day-surgery, just a minor affair. Uncomplicated—in and out.

Uncomplicated? If that was the case, why had I developed complications? I woke up to a throbbing metronome keeping time in my lower back, each beat hitting me harder than the last.

Adding to my distress, my roommate was suffering from an intestinal illness. Mom and Dad came back from a trip to Juneau to find their daughter in the hospital again. Mom viewed the unsanitary conditions of the fetid room and insisted on a private room for her daughter. After that I enjoyed a quiet room for the rest of my extended stay. My boyfriend Mike came by to visit often but could do nothing to ease my pain. My co-workers from downstairs came up to offer their condolences—to see for themselves that I wasn't upstairs sneaking a puff. Once recovered from that surgery I felt no relief from my original complaints. My swollen tummy and abdominal pain grew worse each day.

I worked at the hospital for a while longer, but I'd spent enough time on the set of my own soap opera, and eventually decided to hang up my scrubs for good.

Chapter 7

Mike set the tone for our relationship. He enjoyed quiet evenings at home and had no interest in wining and dining with my friends. He thought I was a social butterfly who was only interested in flitting from soiree to soiree. I actually enjoyed both scenarios, but quickly learned the social outings would be on my own.

What our relationship lacked in the social arena we made up for with family Scrabble battles around the dining table. We spent hours filling the board, coming up with clever multi-point words with my mom and dad. Mike, always full of blarney, placed wooden tablets of nonsense on the board and dared us to challenge them. When Mom and I tired of the shenanigans, Mike and Dad pulled out the cribbage board, each trying to avoid the stinkhole. Mike loved to tease my parents and he enjoyed an easy camaraderie with them.

We also spent time with his folks who lived at a logging camp on Prince of Wales Island. Mike maintained their house in Ketchikan while they were gone and when they came to town to restock supplies, we gathered around the table swapping stories. His mom kept the coffee flowing, his dad kept the banter going, Mike joined in, and I tried to find my place among them. They seemed to accept me into their fold of redheads, and the subject increasingly turned towards marriage. Mike and I shared a common August 7 birthday and his mother, sisters, and I were surprised when the little velvet box containing my birthday present revealed a sparkly ruby and diamond *necklace*, but no ring. He told everyone he had me on the five-year plan. I met him in 1981—I still had three years to go.

Sensing my impatience with "The Plan" Mike walked me down to Bugge Beach on a chilly December night, as the moon was high and reflecting off the water, and quietly slipped a ruby and diamond ring on my finger. No pomp and circumstance. No big production. No witnesses. I accepted the ring and we both accepted a union of opposites.

Treading Water

The painful, abdominal swelling never subsided, but since no one else seemed concerned, and I was busy planning a wedding, I tried to ignore the discomfort. My clothes were always uncomfortably tight, no matter how many calories I counted. A doctor recommended diuretics, suggesting I eat very little for the first day and drink plenty of liquids. I went to Mike's house and took my first dose of them. Feeling woozy, I fell asleep on the couch. My hands were shaky when I woke up, and my body felt anchored to the cushions, as my head floated away like a hot air balloon. I snuck into the kitchen for a quick snack of Pilot Bread, hoping it would bring my head back to earth.

I woke up on Mike's kitchen floor, bruised, sore and clinging to my cracker. My tiniest Levi jeans didn't resist when I buttoned them, but my muscles had cramped so severely I could hardly walk. I had no idea what diuretics do to electrolytes and that my potassium levels could drop dangerously low. The diuretics took care of water-retention and kept my weight down, but the revolving bathroom door was too inconvenient, so I'd flushed all the pills before the wedding.

We set the wedding date for the following August. Mike's proposal may have been unpretentious, but my wedding plans included a celebration with a room full of people. Mom and I met with photographers, caterers, florists, soloists, and booked our flight to Seattle to select the perfect gown. We zoomed all over Seattle, from one bridal shop to another, from downtown to Bellevue and everywhere in between. I tried on yards of satin and lace, but each gown was too sophisticated, too flowerchild, too tight in the bodice, or just not me. We had almost given up when I remembered reading about a shop in Edmonds in one of the bridal magazines stacked on the floor next to my bed.

We found peau de soie elegance in Edmonds. A dress hidden in a back room of cast-offs with millions of buttons down the back, a deep V in the front, delicate netting at the bodice, that fit beautifully. The only catch was the deep V was a bit too deep, and the slightest bit risqué. It had been hanging on the clearance rack for that very reason. Determined to find a solution, a kind seamstress found the smallest bit of lace that matched the appliqué on the skirt and glued it over the lowest part of the V.

I was excited about my dress, but not about my glasses poking through my veil. After sixteen years of hiding behind thick lenses, I was thrilled when my eye doctor said I would be able to wear contacts. I couldn't wait to see what I'd look like from farther than three inches from the mirror. With jellyfish shaped contacts floating on my eyeballs, I danced out of the vision clinic with my new and improved eyesight and saw the rain in all of its grandeur for the very first time. I ducked in and out of local shops without my glasses fogging up. I leaped over mud puddles and sang in the rain. Oh, the things I could do with my hair now, and how much nicer my veil was going to look, and if only those nasty boys could see me now. My zeal was contagious and Elaine, the gal who sold me my sight, became a lifelong friend.

Sea of Well Wishers

Mom and Grandma had everything under control on my wedding day. My sole duty was to relax on the back deck and watch my nail polish dry.

As Nancy did the honors of fitting hundreds of pearl buttons into tiny loops it was apparent my dress was too tight. My scale hadn't reflected any weight gain but all my clothes felt snug in the midriff lately. The waist-cinching dress I'd worn the night before had been unbearable by the end of the evening, and my stomach still ached from the pressure. With no time for Cinderella-type modifications, I pulled my veil over my face, placed my arm in Dad's and began the slow approach into my new life, hoping I wouldn't pop any buttons on the way to the altar.

Twilight sunbeams filtered through stained glass windows bathing the sanctuary with soft light. Candles, salal, and roses filled the room with a potpourri of confusing scents, and Bach's, *Jesu, Joy of Man's Desiring* set the pace as I floated down the aisle. My white dress and dusty rose bouquet complemented my groom dressed in gray. I handed off my bouquet and glanced at Mom who was quietly dabbing at tears. Mike stepped down and offered his hand, relieving Dad of his duties.

After exchanging our vows, we skipped down the stairs of the First Lutheran Church as gonging bells announced our nuptials. Somehow, I had managed to get this self-proclaimed bachelor to abandon his five-year plan of "we'll see" to marry me. The reception was a blur of champagne punch and well-wishers.

We celebrated our mutual birthday three days later as a married couple in Hawaii. We drove the roller coaster Hana Highway on Maui, took an evening cruise on a catamaran, and then explored the wonders of the Big Island. It was lovely vacation full of laughter and joy, but as we playfully jumped through soothing bath temperature surf a storm was brewing on the horizon.

A Storm's a Brewin'

We'd been married for seven months and were busy setting up our little home with our hundreds of wedding gifts. The best gift of all was the one we bought ourselves, a huggable German Schnauzer puppy we named Teddy. Though he didn't have a car seat, Teddy's nose prints on the passenger side window and paw prints on my pants proved he was our baby.

Things should have been great. I'd married the man of my dreams and we enjoyed our cozy home just beyond Bugge Beach. I loved my new job at the vision clinic working alongside my new friend Elaine. Mike and I laughed and shared stories every Friday evening with one of his groomsmen and his wife Charm. By all appearances, things looked fine as we buzzed all over town in our dilapidated blue Chevette, but the honeymoon was over.

The wedding preparations, honeymoon in Hawaii, and settling into our new life had been a distraction from my ailments, but it wasn't long before the pain and bloating became difficult to ignore. The typical winter wardrobe for a fashion conscious gal was pantyhose, half-slip, fitted skirt or dress with pronounced waistline, and a belted wool coat. Pantyhose are tight on a good day, adding a few more waist-cinching items and trying to tame my distended tummy was impossible. Everyday my stomach swelled like bread dough, alleviated only by lying down and going to sleep as soon as I was home from work.

Rolls of do-not-leave-home-without-them antacids filled the bottom of my purse and the console of the Chevette. The chalky antidotes had accompanied me on my Hawaiian honeymoon, an integral part of my trousseau, but for all my consumption of the minty pills, I never felt relief. With the promise of spring, and after peeling off several layers of clothing, my swollen abdomen emerged from hiding. Reluctantly, I conceded it was time to bring my discomfort out of hibernation and visit my doctor again.

My feet had worn a hole through the padded stirrups at my general practitioners office and he finally referred me to a gynecologist. I exchanged formalities with the new doctor, and after he had done the requisite pelvic exam he asked why I was there. I retold my woeful tale and he sent me on my way without answers. My patience waned after repeated visits to report increased pain. I was tired of patronizing pats on the knee, or antibiotics for non-existent urinary tract infections. I needed real answers and real action. The conversation at my next visit went something like this:

"My stomach hurts all the time. Sometimes I can hardly breathe."

"Mm, hm."

"It swells so badly after I eat I can't button my pants, even if I eat something as mundane as soup."

"Hm." The doctor put on his readers and started to thumb through my records.

"I just got married last August and the honeymoon is definitely over. I am in so much pain I can't stand to be touched."

I don't recall exactly what he said next, but it alluded to "female problems."

I rejected his theory. Obviously I was a female with a problem, but his gynecologic expertise had taken on a cynical tone. He may have had years of experience, but clearly couldn't empathize with my "female problems." The closest he might come is if my foot slipped its stirrup and kicked him in the groin.

I mentioned a laparoscopy but he was dismissive. I gathered my paper gown about me and reminded the doctor I knew what a laparoscopy was because as he could see from my scars I'd had previous surgeries, including a ruptured appendix which was discovered through the laparoscope and operated on by him and my regular doctor. I was willing to bet the laparoscope would reveal something this time too. In exasperation, I began my diatribe:

"People think I'm making up symptoms. They think I'm a hypochondriac. I'm so tired of defending myself and being in pain. I just got married last summer and this should be the happiest time in my life. Sometimes I feel like blowing my f**king head off."

He capitulated—if for no other reason than to get the raving lunatic out of his office.

I can't remember telling Mike about the scheduled laparoscopy. My ailments were frustrating for both of us and he spent even more time shaking his head and smoking his pipe.

Malignant-Sea

The laparoscopic journey to the center of my innards revealed a *massive* surprise.

Excerpts from hospital notes, March 18, 1985:

This patient has recently been having crampy abdominal pain with a lot of pain when her bladder is full. The pain limits the amount her bladder can hold. Serial urinalysis were normal. Cystoscopy was normal and the adhesions to the dome of the bladder were found by laparoscopy by Dr. _____ last week.

Just ten days later I was back in the OR. My doctors partnered in Operation Save Rebecca.

Mrs. McCormick is a young woman patient of ours for the last 15 years, who is admitted because of pain and urinary symptoms, specifically small bladder, urgency and pain when her bladder is full. She has had a recent history of apparent urinary tract infections treated in our office by antibiotics and in 1978, an appendectomy by me for acute appendicitis. Ten years ago I did a resection of an inflammatory process of the left carotid (sic), which was benign and not a tumor. Dr. _____ did a laparoscopy ten days ago to try to explain the pelvic pain, and found a dense omental adhesion to the top of the bladder, etiology of which is unclear at this time. It does, however, explain her symptoms very well and the patient is being admitted for exploration and removal of this dense adhesion through Pfannenstiel incision.

My years of complaints were legitimized. My whining justified. My pain unimagined. My integrity restored.

I woke to a room awash in flowers, cards, and visitors—a buffer between the rigors of abdominal surgery. Elaine came to my bedside and told me I had "good color" which was hilarious, given my washed out gown, my washed out complexion, and the lovely orange walls. I got the giggles, which hurt like hell.

I'd endured a whopping amount of just-this-side-of-dead anesthesia in the last couple weeks, but now that the adhesions were gone I looked forward to a new pain-free life. I had lost a few pounds and I was delighted that when the swelling went down I would be able to wear some skinny clothes that had been hanging out in the back of my closet.

About a week after the second surgery, I was back at work making sure eyeglass temple screws were tight enough before dispensing them to patients. I wasn't enthused about pushing a cart around the grocery store after working all day, so I called Mike to see if he wanted to stay in town for dinner. I don't recall our conversation exactly, but it went something like this:

"Hello?" There was hesitancy in his response.

"Hi, I thought maybe we could stay in town and have some fried rice."

I heard a heavy sigh. "Not tonight, Beck."

"Why?" I stood in the back room and began to get annoyed that Mike was not going to help me blow my new found waist-line.

"Huh?"

Now there was a clue. Mike always said "huh" when he was buying time. He was hiding something from me.

"Come on, sweet and sour sauce. You know you love it."

"No."

No? Did he say no? This never went over well. I wondered what his problem was. "Why not?"

Elaine came in the back room and I began to fidget because I should have been working.

"Beck, I have a meeting."

"Some sort of work thing?"

"Not exactly."

Slowly it began to dawn on me—this secrecy—if it was work related, or if he didn't want dinner, he wouldn't be acting so weird. He wouldn't be buying time. He'd be laughing by now if I'd caught him in a surprise for me.

There was something else going on. I started to feel electrical impulses under my skin as itchy red spots grew on my neck. This had something to do with me. Something big. I dropped the eyeglasses I'd probably bent by that point and sat on the swivel stool.

"Mike, who's the meeting with?"

"Huh?"

"What's going on?" The tone in my voice warned Elaine things were serious.

"I'm meeting with your doctor."

"WHAT?"

"At five o'clock. I have a meeting with your doctor."

"Pick me up at a quarter till. I'm coming along."

Stage III Papillary Serous Adenocarcinoma

The details are sketchy, but the clinic staff looked concerned as the nurse invited us to sit in an office instead of an examining room. I sat next to Mike and stared at official certificates and paintings hanging on the wall of the dark office. My family doctor came in, sat down at his orderly desk, and attempted to tell me I had cancer—Ovarian Cancer. I thought I saw a hint of tears in his eyes as he explained he had been in touch with an *Oncologist*—a new word I would begin to know well—whose recommendation was I fly immediately to Seattle, Washington to meet with him. I asked my doctor a few questions about what he thought I should do. He recommended I get on the plane.

Excerpt from Official Report from my hospital Discharge Summary for the surgery I had on March 18, 1985.

Mrs. McCormick was admitted for lysis and removal of omental adhesions to the peritoneum over the dome of the bladder. The etiology of these adhesions at the time of the procedure were obscure. There was no evidence of significant adhesive process around the appendix which had been ruptured and operated by myself and Dr. _____ about five years ago. The adhesions were cleared and adjacent omentum resected to preclude this happening again. Dr. _____ had discovered this as a source of her problem explaining the bladder discomfort in the presence of normal urines by laparoscopy about a week before. The patient was discharged with a clean wound without difficulties. The pathology yesterday reported adenocarcinoma involving the omental surface, probably from an ovarian source. Both of us examined the uterus and the ovaries grossly and they appeared to be normal. This patient then would appear to have a tiny primary in one ovary metastatic already to the omentum and following appropriate consultation, which is in progress with the tumor service gynecologic oncology people in Swedish. Will undoubtedly need to have a hysterectomy, bilateral salpingo-oophorectomy and by(sic) on chemotherapy for the next year if a cure is to be effected.

I wasn't shocked. I had been sick for a long time and had suffered through enough surgeries that I was beyond the point of surprise. I didn't cry. I couldn't really feel anything. I watched the windshield wipers slap away drops as we drove to my parents' house to tell them the news.

Nothing could have prepared me for the reaction of my folks. Dad said there must have been a mistake and Mom broadcast the news to her friends, the pastor, the church, and the prayer chain. It took about an hour before the entire community was informed.

Telling Mike's parents was entirely different. They wanted me to keep it quiet. Within hours I was living in a dark comedy under a gag order. I hadn't even started the ordeal yet and I was already feeling the tug in too many directions. I spit out the gag, drove to Elaine's house, and spoke for myself.

As the last gongs of the wedding bells echoed above the Tongass Narrows the death knell of ovarian cancer attempted to chime in.

Granting No Quarter

That night I let Mike hold me and we both cried—it seemed like the appropriate thing to do, but my tears felt manufactured. I was stoic but tried to feel something: sadness, anger or grief, but all I felt was vindication. I'd had support from close friends and family, but other folks had been cruel to me. They'd doubted not only my intentions but acted as if I was making up stories. I shook the hypochondriac albatross from around my neck and relished my "I told you so" moment. But the price for vindication was steep.

Cheery flowers showed up on my stoop and my phone jangled for days. It was amazing how fast the malignancy spread through the phone lines and up and down Tongass Avenue. I may as well have hung a banner over the tunnel as folks in Ketchikan do whenever a big event is happening.

In the midst of the chaos, I was also bird and dog sitting for Charm and her husband while they visited family in Juneau. Mike had taken the birds to the basement because their screeching kept me awake while I was recovering from my surgery. I found them—claws facing towards heaven—dead in their cage. Apparently, they had gotten too cold. After wrapping them in fabric softener sheets and carefully placing them in their static-free coffin, I buried them in the back yard under an evergreen tree.

As if killing two birds wasn't enough, while I was burying my feathered friends, Charm's dog got loose. We lived mere feet from the busy road and I was terrified the dog would be run over by a car. At this point, one day before I was to fly south to learn if I was destined for the same fate as the birds, and while Mike was patrolling South Tongass Highway looking for the missing mutt, I grabbed for the first thing within reach and threw a wooden spoon across the room. Its impact was minimal. I wanted to smash all my china into pieces and open the windows and tell the world how mad I was, but I didn't. I had this private, short-lived moment of insanity alone. Mike returned about an hour later with the delinquent dog. For the evening, at least, everything was right in my world.

Morning came fast and there was little time to contemplate. I curled my hair and talked to Teddy as I waited for Mike to load the car. Mom, Mike and I sat together on our flight to Seattle, each lost in our thoughts—each mentally preparing for the next day.

Chapter 8

On the morning of April 2, 1985, about fourteen days since my last surgery, I sat in the reception area of the clinic that specialized in gynecology and oncology. Pacific Northwest and Alaskan paintings offered familiarity to an otherwise foreign setting. My nervous chatter, the background elevator music, constant ringing of phones, and occasional unchecked laughter of the girls behind the counter, broke through the understood silence. Mom, Mike and I sat there for an eternity as the second hand on the wall clock refused to pick up pace. Everyone spoke in hushed tones until at almost perfect intervals a chipper nurse poked her head out of the backroom of secrets, breaking the silence.

I tried to eavesdrop on whispered conversations. Did everyone else in the waiting room have cancer? Were they there to hear their baby's heartbeat for the first time? Were they going to die?

What was taking so long?

It felt like the last day of second grade as one-by-one everyone passed through the door but me.

Was I about to hear, "Rebecca, your organs are faulty. You have failed Reproductive Organs Class 101."

Each time the nurse popped out and called a name my heart jumped. I began to thumb through magazines, trying to concentrate on stories about celebrities whose lives were in turmoil over ratings, million dollar contracts, or the latest hairstyle, but concentration was impossible. I was in hyper-speed and could not stop talking. Mike was no doubt wishing for a smoke, while the slightest movement in Mom's lips indicated silent prayer.

"Rebecca?"

Finally, Miss Chipper summoned us to the chamber of answers. I fully expected her to escort us to an examining room, but we had the dubious honor of meeting the oncologist in his office. Suddenly people were taking me seriously. I would never again be the chronic, whining patient, reciting ailments to a doctor eager to treat someone with a *real* illness. I'd gained credibility and now held the gold card to the medical elite.

Red Sky at Morning

The oncologist told me I had what appeared to be ovarian cancer and that the Tumor Board had met to discuss my case. I wondered if the board discussed everyone who was diagnosed with cancer. Apparently, cancer had infiltrated microscopic cells throughout my abdomen to throw the experts off track, patiently waiting to claims me as its next victim. I'd been tough to diagnose for a couple reasons: a) my complaints, while always related to abdominal pain were not specifically related to my ovaries; and b) my age was working against me because the disease was not typically considered for the pre-menopausal population.

Apparently, the Tumor Board had reached an impasse. I presented as a 24-year-old woman in the first months of her honeymoon who had never had children—saving my ovaries was paramount. At the same time I was a 24-year-old facing a life-threatening disease who might not live long enough for it to matter. The conservatives cast their ballot for immediate surgery (a staging laparotomy) to decrease the chance of death-by-reproductive-system—and possibly the chance of ever reproducing. The liberals rallied support for tabling the surgery for six months to see if chemotherapy would be the cancer's grim reaper.

I aligned myself with the liberals and signed on for round one of chemotherapy.

Excerpt from oncologist's letter to family doctor, April 2, 1985:

I discussed with them the options available to us at this time including staging laparotomy followed by treatment based on the findings at that time or primary chemotherapy followed by a second look staging laparotomy after six courses of treatment. I emphasized that we would be making two assumptions were we to pursue the latter course. The first assumption is that there is residual disease left in her abdominal cavity and the second assumption is that there is nothing left in her abdominal cavity which would progress over the next six months under the influence of triple drug cytoxic chemotherapy. I indicated to them that I was comfortable with those two assumptions and would be willing to proceed should they concur. The entire family understood that the chemotherapy carried with it some risk and similarly understood that tumors of low malignant potential might not respond to chemotherapy at all.

After a thorough discussion of these sticky questions, she was admitted to the hospital and given her first course of triple drug chemotherapy using Cytoxan 750 mg per m2, Adriamycin 50 mg per m2, and Cis-Platinum 50 mg per m2. Her body surface area was calculated at 1.6 square meters. She tolerated the first course without difficulty and should be ready for her next course in approximately three weeks' time.

Until that meeting, "chemotherapy" was not even in my vocabulary. There was no way in hell I understood what was in store for me, but I'm sure I nodded and smiled appropriately from the other side of the oncologist's desk. I was on a people mover stopping at information stations along the path, where experts told me things, but I had no point of reference to pose intelligent questions, and there was no time for them to explain the details. I had the choice of checking into the hospital then, or waiting until the next morning. I may not have felt well-informed but I knew for sure I didn't want Mike and Mom in the room during my treatment. They were already getting on my nerves, each one trying to comfort me—Mike with pained silence or jokes, and Mom with feeble prayers. The last thing I needed was for them to be hovering over me. No one knew how to act and if I was going to be sick or in pain or terrified, I didn't want to share the experience with anyone.

Maelstrom

I checked into my room on the beautiful cancer ward. It felt like a penthouse for only the most privileged patients. The colors were reminiscent of my wedding palette of eight months before—cool burgundies and soothing mauves. The hushed tones and sympathetic faces of the visitors we passed in the plush waiting room indicated things were serious on the mauve and burgundy wing.

When I arrived in my room, I exchanged awkward formalities with a woman who was packing a small overnight bag. She wore a blue turban, and a few wiry tufts of drab silver peeked out at the nape of her neck. She looked like she'd just fought multiple rounds in the ring. It was clear the opponent had done some damage.

It dawned on me I was about to do battle in an unfair fight. I wasn't prepped. I had no coach. I'd forgotten to pack my boxing gloves, and I was about to send my support team away.

After Mom and Mike said their reluctant goodbyes, a long-haired pretty nurse gave me a Valium, and began the long process of hydration to protect my kidneys and other internal organs before the chemotherapy. Unlike Miss Chipper, she was gentle and subdued. Her concerned whispers were an ominous foreshadowing of what the next hours would bring. Afraid to show fear, I smiled while my knees knocked under the covers.

After six hours of intravenous hydration, the nurse hung the first bag of my triple cytoxic cancer eradicators—bleach, detergent, and stain remover. I knew the chemicals found their mark when I felt a burning sensation between my legs. I was in a wash machine, sloshing round and round, while the *new and improved three-times-stronger* scoured the cancer stain.

I spent hours doubled over my pillow as my stomach rejected the potent triple threat. Disoriented and dizzy I lost track of my call button and could not reach the emesis basin before I threw up all over myself. When the pretty nurse came back to my room, she changed my gown and spent the rest of her shift cupping an emesis basin under my chin.

Not eager to recount the night's events, I mustered a brave front for Mike and Mom the next morning. It's laughable to read in my medical records that I "tolerated the first course without difficulty."

Nancy lived in Seattle now and she invited us to stay at her place while I tried to recover. I crawled into her bed and pulled the duvet to my chin, making sure a bowl was close by. The spin cycle had left me wrung out like a damp towel that hadn't been pulled from the washer—stretched and crackly. I was exhausted and all I wanted to do was sleep.

My brother Mike and my grandparents showed up and I could hear them talking quietly outside the door. I hadn't seen my grandparents since my wedding but I was not well enough to socialize. Nancy made crinkly chocolate cookies for her guests but I had a sudden aversion to the smells wafting from the kitchen. As guests gobbled cookies, I threw up chemicals.

I don't remember much about those couple days at Nancy's place except Mike and I had started arguing. He was undoubtedly scared and wanted to comfort—and be comforted—by his wife, but I'd been transported to a new reality and there was only room for me.

Having recently visited a scissor-happy beautician who chopped my hair so viciously it reminded me of my dreaded pixie haircuts, I didn't shed any tears when Nancy and my entourage went to Southcenter Mall in search of the perfect wig. My legs ached terribly and I was still weak from the chemotherapy treatment, and I toted a little bowl around in a plastic bag just in case I felt the need.

I tried on long blonde wigs, short auburn wigs, straight, curly, and brunette wigs. Nancy and I were cracking jokes about a deep red wig that would solidify my standing in the McCormick clan, much to the displeasure of the clerk who thought we were just goofing around. Just when she was ready to reprimand her noisy patrons, she noticed Mom and Grandma dabbing at their tears. When it dawned on her

I *needed* wigs, she became most helpful. After much preening in front of the mirror, I selected three winners—two brunette beauties with cascading curls I called my *Loretta Lynns*, and another red one I called *Little Orphan Annie*, bought in honor of all the redheads in Mike's family.

Rebecca L. Durkin

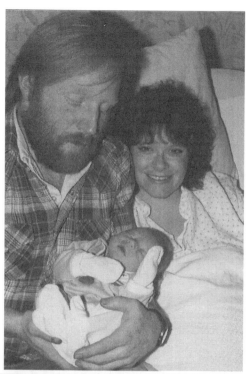

Rebecca L. Durkin

Chapter 9

Mike bought me a sheer floral wrap dress for Easter, which I wore in the uncomfortable tubular confines of the 737. Eight months ago we were a giddy couple returning from our honeymoon, eager to begin our new married life. There was no giddiness as Mike pulled the seat-back tray down and started writing notes in a cancer support booklet someone gave him at the hospital:

April 7

Flying home from Seattle. Becky still acts like she doesn't know what's going on. But I'm scared. I look over at her and she's smiling, happy go lucky. I really don't know what I'll do without her. I will always love her forever.

The plane touched down on Gravina Island as Easter Sunday church bells beckoned from the other side of Tongass Narrows. We pulled our luggage off the belt, and I tried to keep up with Mike as we hurried down the ramp to catch the airport ferry. We waited in line at the tollbooth as wind ripped through our clothes, rain pelted our faces, and I not so silently cursed the wisdom of building the airport on the other side of the Narrows. It would take me years to figure out that fancy dress for arrival in Ketchikan was a lesson in futility, especially when high winds unwrap your fashion statement.

It seemed I was always in recovery mode on Easter Sunday, and I remembered Mom reading *All Creatures Great and Small* after my tumor surgery years before. Easter—the celebration of Jesus rising from the dead, a huge smile on a pastor's face as the church congregation swelled to amazing proportions, children tugging at uncomfortable finery while dragging around baskets of candy, and crying into their big stuffed bunnies during the entire sermon. For me Easter was symbolic of cheating death and feeling like crap.

Mike insisted we visit his parents as soon as we arrived in Ketchikan. I hadn't recovered from the ravaging effects of the chemotherapy, and my legs still ached and felt like lead. I had never felt as tired as when I trudged step-by-never-ending-step up the hillside. I was not ready to face my in-laws. I guessed they would have a lot to say about the cancer situation. My linguistic backhand, weakened by current events, had me fearing my humorous deflecting techniques would not be able to keep up with their questions. It was stressful to report on all that had happened in the last few weeks, and I was not ready to discuss the ramifications of cancer and chemotherapy on my life or possible heirs to the throne.

A few days after my return from Seattle, my old friend Tammie's mom called to tell me she'd baked me a pie to cheer me up. She said she'd been praying and was sure I would be okay. She was fighting her own battle with liver disease and said she was not afraid of what was happening to her and that she was at peace. To comfort me with one of her pies, as she was literally in the last days of her life, was vintage Shirley Taylor. She died later that year, but knowing she was at peace and remembering her courage and golden smile made it easier for me to face my illness.

Crew Cut

I was visiting with Charm when it happened. I took a sip of my coffee, tucked my feet underneath me and ran my fingers through my hair. As Charm rounded the corner with her cup, I held up a fistful of fine brown strands.

Charm asked what she could do. I think I asked for a lint brush or some other snarky comment. I'm not sure she appreciated my caustic humor. I had already killed her birds and almost lost her dog, and now she was the one to share in my hair loss.

Charm watched as I sat trance-like, pulling out clumps. I suppose I wasn't acting in a predictable fashion but there was no way I could mourn the terrible haircut. I laughed deep belly laughs until she had no choice but to join me as my hair embedded itself in her carpet.

For days I shed hair like a shaggy mutt. Fine silky strands accumulated in corners and morphed into giant dust bunnies. As more hair fell, I wondered if there was a can of drain cleaner big enough to take care of the resultant hair clog. I finally set a chair in the center of our kitchen, handed the scissors to Mike and had him cut off the remaining tufts.

A week or so later I took my wigs into the salon for a trim. I'd been wearing my *Loretta Lynns*, but I had to admit Nashville style looked out of place in Alaska. The hairstylist took a little gadget and secured the wig to my head like a party hat. She dabbed away her tears before she transformed *Loretta* to better suit Rebecca.

Skull & Crossbones

One morning in late April 1985, the shrill alarm began beeping around three o'clock in the morning and I wondered why I had waited for it to jolt me into the day. I'd been lying awake for hours. Mike took Teddy outside while I shuffled into our little bathroom, shivered, hopped into a warm shower and got ready to face my second chemotherapy treatment.

I shifted my weight on the bathroom counter and continued my new routine: I applied blusher to colorless cheeks, carefully drew eyebrows where once there had been at least a sparse amount of down, and meticulously worked my mascara wand to enhance the few remaining lashes left rimming my now, in contrast, amazing blue eyes.

I pulled my wig off the Styrofoam mold, shook off the dust, and strategically placed it on my head. Perfection. I leaned down and gave Teddy a kiss as Mike and I headed out the door.

I clutched my coat tight against the cold rain outside, grateful for the warmth of my wig. The streetlights cast a ghost-like appearance around the tunnel in downtown Ketchikan, while the rain falling like unending teardrops seemed to fit the dismal zone I would soon enter.

My doctors at the hospital in Seattle had informed those in Ketchikan of the proper protocol. I checked in promptly at four o'clock in the wee hours of the morning, expecting the same type of treatment I'd received in Seattle a few weeks before.

Rather than guiding me to the elevator for a lift to the second floor, I soon learned the hospital staff wasn't planning to admit me. I was supposed to breeze through eighteen hours of hell and march out of there as a normal out-patient. But I wasn't normal. I believe I was the first, or one of the first, to endure this particular regimen in Ketchikan. I adjusted my wig in silent indignation and plastered a smile to my lips, not letting on for a second that I'd expected anything else. The desk clerk gave me my walking papers to the ER where a nurse greeted me and pointed out a curtained cubicle with a two-foot wide gurney.

I trussed myself tight in the drab hospital dress, applied another layer of lipstick to compensate for the gown, and hoisted myself atop the black plastic cot. The curtain remained open as ER activity revolved around me.

"Hi Rebecca," whispered a lab tech I knew from church. She drew my blood and looked as if she was about to cry as I smiled at her reassuringly.

"Hi Becky," A previous co-worker from my earlier days as chief bottle washer at the hospital brought me a cocktail of cranberry juice and ginger ale.

I felt pretty good at this point and wished I could have been dressed in something nicer for my guests.

"Heya Becky, how you doing?" said another acquaintance as the ER nurse started me on a fast drip of intravenous hydration with Mannitol to suspend my organs. The hydration felt like Niagara Falls as I repeatedly barreled to the can with the IV pole in tow.

Mike sat in the corner of the room trying to read a magazine and escape from the bizarre ritual that was about to take place.

Mom showed up looking somber, and jockeyed for a comfortable position on an orange vinyl chair. Since I hadn't allowed her or Mike to witness my first chemo treatment neither one of them knew what to expect. Mom appeared apprehensive, which seemed to annoy stiff upper-lipped Mike. Soon her knitting needles were clickety-clacking as she concentrated on the bed jacket she was convinced I'd need and tried her darndest to conceal her tension.

At shift change, another round of well-wishers peeked around my curtain while I sat crossed-legged in the middle of the gurney and tried to maintain my cheery persona while checking out the menu.

Not one for breakfast cuisine, I decided to skip that course and go straight to lunch. My tray overflowed with goodies from the kitchen: Jell-O, bullion, coffee, juice, Salisbury steak, and spicy chicken soup with crackers.

Everyone that went in and out of the ER that day could see me, and the ER was busy. After six hours of hydration, a nurse administered the first of the triple cytoxic cocktail. The drugs had been flowing through my veins for about an hour when another nurse arrived on the scene and assessed the situation. She seemed alarmed as she checked my pulse and blood pressure and started adjusting things on the IV pole, all the while muttering about proper protocol and piggybacking the medicines—terms unfamiliar to me.

The nurses began to argue about the danger of the procedure and the importance of the protocol, both asserting themselves as the authority. A turf war ensued. Tension hung as heavy as the toxic bags on the IV pole.

Sweat beads dotted my upper lip and shock waves rippled through my body as my heart pounded against my clammy chest. The horrific chemicals were supposed to save me but beyond the fabric curtain it seemed they were discussing my final curtain call. If someone had made a mistake there would be no encore—the chemicals were already decimating everything in their path.

I longed for the calm, pretty nurse from the mauve and burgundy ward.

Mom dropped her needles and knit her brow as worry lines deepened about her eyes. Mike's ruddy complexion turned crimson, and I began to panic and seriously considered yanking the IV's out of my arm and running for the door. With his jaw set and eyes blazing, Mike escorted the nurses away from me and scared them into compliance.

I started feeling nauseous. The room was a tilt-a-whirl and I tried to balance in the center of the cot. My wig was soaked and I quickly discarded it for my stockinet cap (the kind they put on newborns in the OB department). A humbled nurse came to my bedside, replaced the toxic IV bag with another blood-red bag of noxious chemicals, and hung it on the pole. I watched with ghoulish fascination as the red liquid snaked its way to my arm inducing instant vomiting, and instant regret over the spicy chicken soup.

Monitors beeping, sirens whirring, ER staff laughing, Mom praying, Mike pacing, the room spun faster as the chemotherapy waged war against the cancer.

"Hey, Mike," said Charm's husband as he peered around the curtain.

"What are you doing here?" said Mike, eager for comic relief.

I tried to lift my head to smile at Charm, but the slightest movement induced vomiting. The second hand movement induced vomiting. If someone looked at me sideways, I threw up. I buried my head in my pillow, held my breath, and prayed for it to stop.

The pastor stepped into the crowded area.

"She's not doing so well right now," said Mom.

The men tried to ignore my heaving, as Charm, stalwart as ever, offered to help Mom empty bowls, and the pastor averted his eyes from the pathetic bald girl in the middle of the gurney.

I very kindly asked our friends and the pastor to leave. The blood-red bag had done its damage, another one hung in its place.

A splash of vomit hit Mom's arm and instantly peeled off a layer of skin, as Mike stood by my gurney in helpless horror. Very late that night I checked out of the ER. I threw up all the way home and for days after that's all I did.

Chapter 10

Mike had to work on the days following a treatment so he drove me to my folk's house. Dad didn't visit me during treatments, but because he worked from home he was able to help me through my post chemotherapy days. After snuggling into Mom and Dad's big bed, Dad would check in on me and bring me water. I couldn't tolerate food after a treatment, which made me even weaker, and Dad helped me if I started vomiting. I felt like a little child again when Dad would come downstairs for nighttime prayers. This was something he could do, out of the spotlight with no big production—just quiet, simple caring in his generous way.

After my ER experience, Mom had a little talk to the powers that be about the need for me to be off the gurney and in a real bed with some privacy during a treatment. I went from center stage in ER to having my own private room. She was also determined to handle all things financial and otherwise. I had only been with my insurance company for a short time when I learned about the cancer and they decided it would be in their best interests to deny my coverage. I couldn't fight an insurance company, because I was busy fighting for my life, but Mom could, and she was in need of a victory. She fought for her daughter. She fought a battle she could win. She conquered a patent denial and claimed my coverage through the catastrophic illness clause. Surely, the company could see by the claims that I was living a catastrophe, but it took Mom's powers of persuasion to make them uphold their responsibility.

I needed help but I resented it. I was twenty-four and felt I should be able to handle my own affairs, but I had no how-to book on fighting cancer. The chemotherapy weakened my immune system and I was prone to infection. Mom obsessed about the need for me to be careful while shaving my legs, though I had no hair to shave, and about the danger of burning my wigs, the only hair I had, when I opened the oven door. She wore my illness like a shroud. People asked me how *she* was doing. No one would dare ask me. I reveled in total denial as Mom withered from grief.

I may have been the only one who didn't think the illness was going to get me. Prior to my illness, I'd had no experience with cancer in my family or friendships. I had no point of reference. People who died of cancer were either people I didn't know or were much older than me. Women with ovarian cancer—one of the deadliest cancers —died all the time but I was blissfully unaware.

I had known for a long time that something was wrong. I now had an inarguable reason for my pain and I was happy to give it a name. The word that I was grateful for was a word that struck terror in everyone else. It's possible that the doctors relayed a gloomy outlook but I don't recall being preoccupied with my mortality.

Drifting Away

My second treatment in Ketchikan was destined to be different. I stepped off the elevator into old home week and greeted ward clerks and nursing staff on familiar stomping grounds. The pace was slower on the second floor, and the beds with their automatic comfort switches were an improvement over my stint on the two-foot wide gurney in ER three weeks before. I hopped onto the bed knowing things would be better this time. I had my own room and the best nurse on staff. I felt comfortable with her abilities and was grateful to have someone of her caliber in my corner. She arrived at my bedside with self-confidence and enthusiasm and I was ready to get the treatment over with.

Her enthusiasm waned after dealing with my decrepit blood veins. Each time she tried to insert the IV into my hand the vein would roll. The chemotherapy had been insidious in its destruction and had severely compromised my blood vessels. The smell of alcohol prep pads hung heavy in the air and after multiple pokes in the top of my hand, my nurse summoned someone from anesthesia for assistance. About fifteen pokes later, the IV was a functional portal for the chemo cavalry.

Mom sat quietly next to my bed in the ever-present sticky vinyl chair knitting another creation to keep me warm. I'm guessing the constant motion was therapeutic for her. I was always cold, and kept Mom busy getting me blankets from the blanket warmer. When I was finally warm, I kicked off the covers and Mom took the opportunity to rub soothing lotion into my feet.

My attentive nurse popped in and out of my room constantly that morning to see how I was feeling. At one point, she put something into my IV that gave me an incredible relaxed feeling. I began to drift away, feeling better than I had in months—all pain was gone and I felt happy. Somehow, I'd floated to the top of the room above a sudden frenzy of activity. Mom dropped her needles as dark horror cast its shadow on her face.

Was I dying? I was not scared.

"Becky." The nurse's lips were moving as she ambled on top of me desperately trying to rouse me.

I smiled and closed my eyes.

She shook me with force. "Becky."

The shock wore off about as quickly as it overtook me. Mom was petrified, but for me it was just one more weird, and alarmingly peaceful, event that happened on a perilously wild ride.

My second session of chemotherapy in Ketchikan ended predictably—throwing up all the way home.

Paddling in Separate Dinghies

Several months after our honeymoon and a few months into my life as a cancer statistic, Mike and I began to witness a rift in our marriage. A small almost invisible fissure threatened an already unstable core. Less than a year after our wedding Mike and I

93

had a completely different set of expectations. He was still on his honeymoon, expecting wedded bliss, but a definite chill had invaded our household. I tossed aside my honeymoon negligees for flannel gowns to match my new knit stocking caps; and Mike was benched when I became bedfellows with lab techs, nurses, doctors, IV bags, and emesis basins. There was no room for another body.

I wasn't feeling very human. My body was breaking down. My body had let me down. My body, in my view, was no longer desirable. Although I wouldn't acknowledge the death factor, I wasn't blind, and the mirror showed a shocking truth. I couldn't explain this to Mike because I didn't understand it myself. I had no say in what happened to me every three weeks at the hospital. I climbed on a sterile bed, pushed a button or two to gain a modicum of comfort as nurses poked needles into my skin and fed me poisons. I yielded to cancer and a medical team who placed me in a chastity belt of pain and chemical horrors in the first year of my marriage. My body was pinched, blistered and painful with gaping wounds that needed bandages and time to heal.

In between chemotherapy treatments, I gained control. My body, for a week or two, was mine. Mine to hate, mine to love, mine to ignore, mine to share.

I was in a battle for my life. A battle fought with caustic humor, denial and anger. All other battles were on hold. I did not have the strength to fight for my marriage. The small fissure was deepening at a slow but steady pace as the rumblings grew increasingly louder.

Casting Lots

I'd been drafted into the Ovarian Cancer Corp. There was no cancer boot camp. No weekend warrior training. This was a hard fought battle in the fallopian trenches where ovarian cancer defined the territorial lines. Speculums and laparoscopes were the Scouts and the Cisplatin, Cytoxan and Adriamycin, with their blanket wipeout ability, were the Agent Orange.

Now that cancer had become common vernacular, I was more aware of others who were also in a fight for their life. I learned I was in league with a phenomenal legion of warriors in Ketchikan. Some of them fought the battle alongside me. Some of them died. I joined a support group for a while but it was difficult to reconcile the luck of the draw in a deadly game. After a while I didn't want to know about anyone else's sickness. It seemed there was no other topic but cancer and I my shoulders slumped under the weight.

I may not have been able to escape my reality but Ketchikan folk offered support with all kinds of surprises. Tammie's sister Lori presented me with my very own embroidered hospital gown so I could be stylish during my treatments. She also helped set up a trust account for me at a local bank, which greatly helped in offsetting some of the enormous travel expenses associated with battling an illness from the rock.

Absolute strangers called me with tips, tricks, ideas, and mystical powers guaranteed to aid my healing. One charming woman called and extolled the virtues of grapes for nausea. Other people insisted wheat tops were the way to go, while others advised me to sack chemotherapy all together and take a more holistic, natural approach to my healing. Then there were the head-straight-to-Mexico, Laetrile advocates. I figured I was on the right track, and even if I wasn't, I was confident no one knew anymore than I did. It seemed to me the whole treatment thing was a crapshoot. People who had cancer died. People who had chemotherapy died. People were dying of cancer everyday—but I did not see myself as one of those people. This cancer was not going to get me and neither was the chemotherapy. I would take the bitter poisons, for better or worse, and time would tell in August if they were working.

I'd tagged my enemy and the chemo was the necessary and insidious agent to annihilate the beast.

Bobbing Back To the Surface

I slept for days after a treatment, but as soon as I had any energy I would don my wig and favorite fuzzy blue angora sweater, slip into my Levis and walk up and down Ketchikan's hills. It was liberating to get out of the house and away from the mind-jangling phone.

Ketchikan was cool and crisp and the air was a refreshing respite. For the first time in years, I had time to walk up and over Water Street to view the Tongass Narrows and watch the floatplanes and soaring eagles. I enjoyed most of my walks alone with my thoughts and dreams.

I also enjoyed taking myself out for lunch. I'd been warned about eating spicy foods. Bland foods would be easier on my mouth because a side effect of the chemotherapy was mouth sores. Eating what I enjoyed was one thing I could control and all I wanted was taco salads. If spicy salsa was to be the final death knell for my withering taste buds, so be it.

Though my walks provided temporary escape, I spent most of my time fighting. I fought the cancer, fought the effects of the chemo, fought to eat what I wanted, and fought to maintain normalcy in my abnormal world. The last thing I wanted to do was fight those I loved the most, but I felt a constant struggle between my husband and my mom. Mike tried to toughen me up and resented the babying I was receiving from Mom. Mom wanted to take care of her baby and resented the tough love I was receiving from my Mike. I needed a bit of both but instead I was the frayed piece of rope in the middle.

Mom took me to Kay's Kitchen for lunch every Saturday where I enjoyed camaraderie with locals. Mike stayed home and enjoyed camaraderie with his Dad. We sought comfort from others but had no idea how to comfort each other.

I felt I had no say in any facet of my life. My health was out of my hands, my married life was listing dangerously, and everyone had an answer.

While I was trying to navigate my marriage, I still had to have my blood tested every three weeks to monitor my white blood cell count. After about three treatments, a nurse asked me what method of birth control I was using. I'd understood the chemotherapy would make me sterile, if not for life, then at least for the duration of the treatments. The nurse took the last-minute opportunity to inform me this wasn't necessarily the case. She insisted that I take a pregnancy test immediately. I took the test and then took a seat in the waiting room to await the results, pondering the impact that a pregnancy might have on Mike and me. If I was pregnant an abortion would be the likely remedy because of the effects of chemotherapy on the fetus. If I was pregnant this may be the only time in my life I would ever be. If I was pregnant would I have to decide whether the fetus' life was more important than my own? How could I weigh the life of the fetus against the cancer killing chemotherapy?

I already bore the humiliation of everyone knowing every little detail about me and I was sure everyone in the waiting area heard the negative results. Not wanting to make a fuss, I thanked her for the news and then hid behind a magazine in an attempt to ignore knowing looks.

During that visit my blood tests revealed an unusually low white blood cell count that was worrisome to my doctor. The low count meant my immune system was wide open for infection and I would have no way of fighting off illness. Cancer was bad enough but the risk of contracting pneumonia, influenza, or whatever bug Ketchikan was hosting at the time could have posed an even bigger threat. It wasn't good news, but I had reason to celebrate. Because the Cisplatin was the likely culprit for my low white count and was the one that required the laborious hours of hydration, I would be able to enjoy a one-hour treatment in the clinic.

It was a joyous day and Mike and I arrived at the clinic grinning like little kids. Just the fact that he was able to be there for the whole treatment was reason for celebration and we were due for something good. Mike kept me laughing by zooming around the room on the doctor's swivel stool and telling corny jokes. We were both relieved that I would be able to forego a week's worth of nausea, and possibly get in a week's worth of work. This reprieve was going to help immensely. I was putting off an essential part of the cure, but I was prepared to make it up some other time. The nurse came in, poked the top of my hand, hung the IV bag that dripped red poisons quickly into my veins, and before we knew it the treatment was over. I hopped off the table feeling rejuvenated. I felt so great we celebrated by skipping into the mall for ice cream: a chocolate, orange blend that melted deliciously on my tongue. Mike was practically dancing a jig—I'd sailed through a treatment. There was promise at the end of the day.

I was barely out of the mall when the evil chemicals punched me in the stomach. I threw up the celebratory orange chocolate ice cream in the parking lot. My skip turned into a gut-holding amble to the Chevette as I heaved in humiliation and sorrow. I set up camp on the couch, stared out my front window at the unending rain, and vomited intermittently for a week. One day while I was recuperating at home, I heard a faint knock on the door. I wrapped my robe tight, pulled my baby cap down over my hairless head and shuffled to the door. I met my neighbor Jody for the first time as she and her young daughter were ironically asking for donations to the cancer society.

As the side effects worsened, I became psychosomatic every time I stepped over the hospital threshold. As soon as the elevator doors closed my stomach started performing gymnastics. I knew it was in my mind, but that didn't stop the woozy feeling. I willed myself not to let it get me, but the hospital smell, the feel of the sheets, the PA system, all contributed to my weakened mental state. Each treatment was more brutal than the one before. I grew weaker as the nausea and fatigue grew worse with each chemo session.

My sister-in-law bought me a Physicians' Desk Reference and I decided to educate myself on the miracle cures of Cytoxan, Adriamycin and Cisplatin. What the book told me about the drugs scared the hell out of me. They had big bold warnings in a box written before the descriptions. I learned that while killing cancer, the drugs could also destroy everything else in their path including my hearing, internal organs, and heart. I didn't appreciate the irony: diagnosis ovarian cancer—cause of death—cardiac arrest. The Adriamycin and Cisplatin seemed to carry the most risks. The warnings went beyond the run-of-the mill circulars of possible side-effects that *might* happen found in boxes of pain medication. These drugs warned of death. They warned of death by negligence. They called for practiced staff trained in the rigors of chemotherapy and a crash cart at the scene. They were not "take two and call me in the morning" type drugs. These were—pump into veins and pray like hell that they kill the cancer and not the victim—type drugs.

They were not benign. They were as malignant as the cancer that was trying to kill me.

I assessed the scene before every treatment to see if a red crash cart was nearby. I suffered many of the debilitating effects of chemotherapy, including excruciating leg pain and restless legs, relentless nausea, hair and possibly a wee bit of hearing loss, but after reading what could have been I'm happy to have survived the ordeal.

Fair Weather Friends

Cancer casts a wide net to ensnare everyone near its victim, including friends. Some friends cup a hand under your chin and gently float you back to safer waters, offering kind reassurances and loving support. Others need to be needed and can't stop themselves from showing up with casseroles, which add to your nausea, or calling on the phone when you haven't slept in days. And some hide, because it's easier than facing your imminent demise. It's easy to understand their fear. By definition, malignant means: *evil in nature, influence or effect; tending to produce death or deterioration; passionately and relentlessly malevolent.*

Another event underscored cancer's reach. I don't recall the details exactly, but an escalating argument with a coworker revealed her resentment of my health, my happy attitude, and the attention I received. She told me of a family member who'd had cancer, never recovered and died. I had already outlived a few cancer-fighting friends and I didn't need someone resenting my resilience, no matter how misplaced her pain.

While some people avoided me, others stepped up with all kinds of cheer-up-Becky surprises. My friend Bonnie often met me for yummy lunches of clam chowder and homemade croutons at the Fireside Restaurant, where we laughed the entire lunch hour. Elaine decided I had endured enough of the afore-mentioned tug of war and invited me to spend a night at her house to get some needed rest. I took her up on the offer. I don't know whether she heard me, but I cried all night. I did not cry for my current situation; to do so would have meant admitting to myself that it was getting to me. I came up with all kinds of other things from my past to cry about: old boyfriends, Slippers, and my Grandma Holman who had died eleven years earlier.

All I wanted was to forget my illness and to enjoy laughter, friendship, and my marriage, but cancer was the talk du jour and it encroached on almost every conversation.

Chapter 11

In August of 1985, Mike and I spent our first wedding anniversary preparing to return to Seattle. Clad in my cytoxic armor, and waving my liberal banner, I was eager to learn if the liberals could claim victory for their decision, or if the cancer was getting closer to claiming another victim. As eager as I was, I dreaded having my stomach cut open again—of relinquishing control to the surgical team. Just four months since my last surgery, and with all the chemotherapy treatments, I was weak and exhausted and angry about having to yield to the knife. I wasn't looking forward to being fastened by staples, of nurses waking me up to check my vitals, of bed pans and emesis basins, but it was necessary to see if the cancer was dead—and for that I was willing to do just about anything.

Mom and I flew down a few days earlier than Mike to enjoy shopping in Seattle. Mom bought me a lovely periwinkle dress that showcased my blue eyes, and then surprised me with tickets to the Seattle Opera House to see Richard Harris perform in Camelot. For a few hours King Arthur, Guinevere, Lancelot and Merlyn, transported us to a kingdom far away from the Swedish fortress on Pill Hill.

I'd been demoted to the urology ward. Urology was lacking in ambience and once again I wished for the finer things on the mauve and burgundy ward.

A nurse came into my room. "HELLO MRS. MCCORMICK,"

I raised my eyebrows, looked at Mom and Mike, and shrugged my shoulders as the nurse busied herself with something in the bathroom.

"Is there anything that I can get you MRS. MCCORMICK?"

"Maybe some cranberry juice and a ginger ale," I giggled.

The nurse stepped out of the bathroom pulled back the curtain and tripped through her apologies.

Apparently, the chart was for another Mrs. McCormick with a hearing impairment. I assured her my ears were fine and hoped they'd clear up the chart confusion before picking up the scalpel.

An orderly wheeled me down to pre-op and once again, I had to surrender my glasses. Pre-op was full of patients lined up on gurneys like cattle awaiting slaughter. Paranoid thoughts entered my mind. What if I was mistaken for the person next to me? What if I came back minus a breast, a leg, or a toe? What if my charts were still messed up?

My mouth was dry, but I could have no drink. An anesthesiologist came in and explained what he was going to do. I didn't care about anesthetic procedure. I cared that I was unable to see and that I was gagging. He gently patted my shoulder, mumbled a kind word or two, and put some potions in my IV. I couldn't make out any faces but I whispered my tail of woe to the man on the gurney next to me. I told him I had cancer. I complained about having had too many surgeries and pain in my young life and then cried myself to sleep.

As I'd been held in suspended animation, the alien green team butchered me. I had a long vertical wound from above my belly button to my pubic bone and they'd dug so deep into my pelvic lymph nodes my thighs ached. I didn't try to hide when a nurse came towards me with a hideously long needle that administered a morphine escape from hell.

Drowning in a Paper Cup

A day or two after my surgery I developed a bowel obstruction. My abdomen was swelling like a hot air balloon—a critical problem that could have serious consequences. I heard a nurse mention an NG tube. I'd stocked the tubes when I worked in Central Supply at the hospital in Ketchikan and knew what this entailed. They were planning to put a tube into my stomach, via my nose. For the first time since I found out about having cancer, I was terrified. Things had definitely been scary of late, but this spiked the terror meter.

I have always been claustrophobic. The thought of shoving a tube in my nose was the realization of a nightmare. To make matters worse the nurses informed me in the morning, but the procedure would not take place until hours later. I had plenty of time to work myself into a panic. The nurses said I would have to be conscious, but they would give me a sedative beforehand. I knew nothing would make it any easier. In the meantime, all I could do was ramble on to my guests about the injustice of the situation.

Nancy, Mike, Mom and my aunt Jean were all witness to my torture. When the nurse came in and began to open familiar packaging, I knew I was going to die. My entire entourage fled, except for Nancy. The nurse gave me a sedative but it hadn't begun to work before she approached my bedside with all of her "kill Becky" paraphernalia. The nurse inched closer to me with the outstretched tube and a little paper cup of water. Another nurse crept to my bedside to assist the snake-wielding devil who intended to shove it into my nose and force me to swallow it. I screamed, fought, and refused treatment just as I had so many years ago when my tantrum resulted in the puff mushroom incident.

Between the two nurses and Nancy, they restrained me and forced me to swallow the tube. Defeated, I lay back on my pillow as they turned on the machine that sucked the green contents of my stomach into a canister for all of my visitors to see. They gave me some spray that was supposed to numb my throat, but it didn't work. It tasted just like that awful banana stuff from the orthodontic visits of yesteryear.

I looked pitiful. My stockinet cap sat atop my bald head, my eyebrows were long gone, white tape attached the tube to my nose, and IV tubing snaked about the perimeter.

I wavered between conscious and semi-conscious for days. One day I woke up and found Mike visiting with an old high school buddy. I hadn't met him before, but judging the sympathetic look on his face, I figured he thought I wasn't long for this earth. Just a year before I'd walked up to the altar as a beautiful bride. Now I looked like I was getting ready to attend my own funeral.

My friend Bonnie was in Seattle with her husband Randy and she came to my bedside with a box stuffed with the zaniest tights I'd ever seen. Plaid tights, striped tights, and polka dot tights, and alongside of them a set of makeup brushes. I smiled wanly behind my masking taped tube as she tried to get me to laugh. After that visit, my nurses tried to make up for the tube assault by applying lipstick and blush to my lifeless face.

We waited days and days for the pathology reports. I had the luxury of morphine sleep, but I'm sure Mike and Mom were anxious to find out which path I would be on next—the road to recovery—or the road to the pearly gates. Finally, we learned the liberals could claim victory. No more chemotherapy and the oophorectomy was on hold. By denying the cancer's death hold, the malignant fingers slowly eased their grip on my ovaries.

No Smooth Sailing

I didn't go home immediately after my release from the hospital. I still had some recovering to do before I could sit comfortably on a plane for an hour and a half. Mike flew back to Ketchikan and Nancy graciously offered lodging at her apartment in West Seattle again. When I felt well enough to go out, Nancy and I decided to play dress up. I wore a royal blue silk dress, tons of makeup, and my wig, while Nancy chose an elegant black and white print wrap dress. After several passes through a decadent dessert bar at a fancy hotel, we visited our favorite pub where a warm reception by the regulars and a couple pints of pear cider offered temporary respite from my condition. I was weak and tired, but it was fun to hang at Murphy's and collect a few compliments from men who were unaware of the stitching and adhesive tape holding me together.

When I had recovered sufficiently I flew back to Ketchikan. When Mike opened the door to our little house in Ketchikan, I walked into a wonderful surprise. He and his mother had completely re-done my kitchen in gleaming parquet wood floor, light pink walls with mauve trim, and one of the walls had the lovely wallpaper on it that I had selected earlier that year. Mike's mom gave us one of her small china cabinets to display all our wedding gifts, and the silver and crystal shone in their proper setting amidst the perfect backdrop.

Navigating New Waters

By September, I was healthy enough for work. I'd lost my job at the eye clinic because I missed so much work, so I approached my former employer at a credit union where I'd worked prior to my illness. I stood proudly behind the counter in my perfect synthetic hair and waited on all of my favorite customers, but I was no longer Becky the friendly teller. I was Becky the teller with cancer.

It seemed everyone that walked into the credit union knew about my illness and my face was set in a plastic smile as I constantly said I was fine. One afternoon a favorite teacher from high school approached the counter. As I processed his transaction, he asked me how I was doing. Assuming he was asking in reference to my illness, I replied I was much better. The look on his face informed me he was unaware of my recent peril and was simply uttering a "how are you?"

I thought everyone knew.

He asked if I'd been ill.

I lowered my voice and told him I had ovarian cancer but that I was in remission.

Tears welled in his eyes as he took both of my hands in his, mentioned a student who had recently died, and said he'd pray for me.

By December I'd regained some of my strength and was looking forward to the annual staff Christmas party. Mike bought me a cardinal red silk dress from a shop called *Her Garment Bag* at Ketchikan's brand new mall. The store was beautiful, and the owners were patient as I spent hours trying on dresses, and actually feeling attractive for the first time in a very long time.

I placed my crowning glory on my head, and Mike and I headed for the party at the Fireside Restaurant. Dinner conversation was lively and soon the music promised dancing. My coworkers took their positions on the floor as I found renewed interest in my cocktail. It wasn't long before my boss's husband made his way behind my chair.

"May I have this dance?"

I concentrated on my drink.

He urged me to join the fun.

"Well?"

I looked beseechingly at Mike who shrugged his shoulders. I looked at all of the people dancing on the floor without difficulty. I picked up my drink and chugged it down. I wondered why I should be afraid. It was time for closure of the ugly duckling era. It wasn't as if I'd be dancing blind, and the only people on the stage were band members. No one was expecting me to pirouette out of the wings. I smiled my sweetest smile, patted my hair, and offered my hand.

I giggled and informed him I was not too good at this. He informed me that I'd just never had a good dance partner and all I had to do was let him lead. Leading me onto the dance floor was one thing, it was just two simple steps down, but leading me in a dance? I was beginning to regret my decision. This was the equivalent of dental visit.

He told me I was doing fine.

Maybe so, but it was probably because of the multiple gin and tonics I'd consumed in anticipation of the dreaded eventuality.

He added some fancy footwork to the repertoire.

All anxiety about my lack of grace subsided when I felt a shift on the top of my head. His wedding ring caught my wig. I had no idea if he knew I wore one. Suddenly I was dancing like a pro, while simultaneously trying to disentangle my hair. I'm fairly certain he knew something was off kilter, but thank goodness it didn't end up being my wig, which saved both of us the humiliation of dancing with the plucked chicken.

Even though I was weak and uncoordinated, Mike and I joined the credit union's bowling league and I may have been the worst bowler ever to step on the lanes. When it appeared we were taking our bowling league duties seriously my parents bought bowling shoes for us. They also gave me a bowling bag. My bag was reminiscent of *The Flintstone's*. It was pewter colored and circular and zipped right around the purple ball. With my big hair and funny bag and Mike's stocky build we looked just like *Betty* and *Barney*. What I lacked in bowling skill, I made up for in laughs and we had a great time hanging out in the smoke-filled alleys with my boss and her husband. One Monday evening, the pure platinum that coursed through my veins must have given me super-human strength, because I miraculously bowled a 192.

Shortly after Christmas, I decided to quit my job. It was always busy with customers and it was hard to wait on people all day. I signed up for unemployment, relieved that I would be able to enjoy some rest and relaxation. I anticipated the checks rolling in as I sat around watching TV and eating Bon Bons. Unfortunately, that pipe dream belonged to someone else and it was clear that we needed more than one income. In less than two weeks, I was offered a teller position by two banks and I had to make a decision between them. I started work immediately and became a prisoner to my teller window.

Bonnie had been urging me to bring my black spiky hair out of hiding and I showed up at my new job without the security of my wig. I looked better, but I was beginning to realize the toll the chemo had taken on my body. The tellers weren't allowed to sit on the stools in our windows—which were apparently there just to taunt us—and the hours of standing caused excruciating pain in my back and legs. I revealed to the head teller I'd been seriously ill recently and that it was difficult to stand all day. Breaks were instituted almost immediately and our comfortable stools became more than window dressing.

I made a few new friends on both sides of the counter through my work at the bank, but Mike had little interest in joining me as I flitted like a butterfly between social events. I also joined the Cancer Society with my mom and attended monthly event planning meetings. Having endured a hellacious year, I was ready for some fun and to make sense of my bout with cancer. Mike had endured a hellacious year and had grown even more reclusive. He didn't stand in my way. I didn't stay home. The rumblings began again and the fissure soon widened into a chasm, but we forged ahead and fought hard to overcome in spite of our difficulties.

Chapter 12

In 1988 I beat my diseased, chemo-soaked, ovaries into compliance by defying the odds and becoming pregnant. Everyone I knew was ecstatic about the baby. While I sat back and enjoyed the gentle roller coaster in my tummy, Elaine hosted a baby shower, Mike's dad built a lovely cradle, mom's knitting needles clicked a happy tune, and the Cadillac of strollers graced my entryway.

The Cancer Society hosted an annual fund raising auction that was held at the bank where I worked that year. Our teller windows became stand-up bars as members of the Bar Association served spirits that loosened tongues, purse strings, and wallets for better auction bidding. With chemotherapy a few years behind me, and pre-natal vitamins doing their thing, my hair was full and luxurious for the first time in my life. As I served cake to party goers, a gracious woman complimented my hairstyle and reached out to touch my luscious locks. I recognized her as the mother of a young girl I'd met at a cancer support group. Her daughter died of leukemia the same year I was having my treatments. Here I was in all of my post-cancer, pregnant glory, serving cake at a cancer society benefit. I felt like a cancer poster child—honored for surviving, living, fighting back. I made a hasty exit, hid in the bathroom, and tried to reconcile why I had been spared in the game of cancer roulette when her lovely daughter had not been so fortunate.

Later that year the Rotarians recognized me as the Most Courteous Clerk, which was almost as good as my Best Citizen of the Fourth Grade award. I waddled onto center stage, my only prop a great big round tummy showing the world this nice gal had kicked the shit out of ovarian cancer.

I was active throughout my pregnancy and worked until the doctor said I had to stop, very near my due date. One morning late in April, I donned my favorite pair of expando jeans and a green and white striped top that accentuated my bowling ball tummy and drove to the same clinic I had visited at the onset of my cancer nightmare. This time gloved hands weren't checking for painful masses. Now the occupant of those gloves measured an abdomen holding the promise of new life that grew more massive with each passing week. After the midwife checked for dilation, she had an odd look on her face and said she'd be right back. My heart thudded as dark thoughts seeped into my mind.

A knock on the door interrupted my thoughts. The midwife stepped in and asked if I'd been feeling any contractions. I told her nothing significant, but that I was a bit uncomfortable. I told her about my long walk the night before and that considering my condition I was actually feeling great.

The midwife smiled and said the baby seemed to be fine. Good heartbeat, no signs of fetal distress.

She told me I was quite dilated.

I sat up a bit taller. I'd read all the horror stories about labor, and the requisite dog-eared copy of *What to Expect When You Are Expecting* graced my nightstand. I knew what was in store for me. Considering the dilation, I should have been feeling significant labor pains by now.

I accepted my good fortune and didn't ask any questions to jinx it. I was about to have a baby and hadn't felt a thing. The midwife said I could either go to the hospital or stick close to town. I could only go so far in Ketchikan anyway.

I eased myself off the table and victory-waddled to the waiting area. Expectant mothers—my comrades in tents—awaited the update as the receptionist began to set my next appointment.

"No need," I said.

Magazines were set aside as all pregnant bellies turned towards me.

I told them I'd be having a baby in a couple hours.

One of the women asked if I was going to be induced.

"Nope."

Thinly veiled skepticism was obvious in the raised eyebrows and knowing looks of mothers who had had the same wishful thoughts.

"I'm already dilated to six centimeters." I didn't ponder how weird it was to announce the size of the opening of my cervix. Pregnancy strips all inhibitions away.

If I could have bowed, or spun a pirouette, I would have.

I decided to wait out the next few hours at Mom and Dad's house while Mike was at work, just in case the baby decided to make its grand entrance with no warning. We sat around and chatted with Mom's neighbor about how lucky I was to be laughing through labor. I finally checked into the hospital at about seven o'clock that evening and Mike showed up soon after.

The midwife appeared an hour or two later and announced that I was even more dilated. I still hadn't been feeling contractions so she decided to break my water. This brought about some degree of normalcy in what was otherwise a fantastically surreal day. Cancer may have pulled my hair out, punched me in the gut, and kicked me in the shins, but a small baby kicked right back.

Small Fry

At 12:19 a.m. on April 19, 1988, Jeffrey Micheal McCormick took center stage.

It was not until the next morning that I started to hurt, and the triangle hanging above my bed revealed its use as I struggled to sit upright. I hadn't felt it when it happened but in Jeffrey's race to the finish line, he had broken my tailbone. I was in great pain but nothing could put a damper on the joyful event. My hospital room was a carnival of activity as visitors revolved through the door. Friends and family were finally able to visit me in a hospital to celebrate a happy occasion. No one struggled for words to say to a sickly bald woman doing her best to comfort her guests. This time I had no gaping wound to keep me from giggling in excitement, and Jeffrey was the only bald one in the room that day wearing a stockinet cap that covered his sweet little cone-head.

The Bitter End

Mike and I had been floating adrift but there was hope that a baby would keep us from going under. Unfortunately, once the umbilical lifeline was snipped and the babe delivered, one more person in the dinghy did not provide the needed stability. We had many happy moments and most of them revolved around our sweet baby boy. But happy moments couldn't make up for years of heartache, sorrow and strife. We had very different ideas of what to do with our lives. We were never free of the threat of cancer, and each time I flew south for exploratory surgery, or had my blood tested for cancer clues it was a reminder of our fate. All of our trips since our honeymoon had been for medical reasons and I was ready to socialize, to take a real vacation, to have a bit of fun with my little family. I needed a break from Ketchikan, but Mike was perfectly content right where he was. He had just started to relax after my cancer fight, and I was restless to celebrate life and get on with things. We drifted further apart, each of us paddling in different directions.

My brother Mike hung his law shingle while I was pregnant and asked if I could help him out after I had my baby. I could run the office while he commercial fished for the summer. I was in no hurry to stand behind a teller line again and this was a great opportunity for me. His law office was right across from City Float and my desk was a fishbowl to all the fishermen below. One of my favorites would occasionally stop by with a non-descript paper bag stuffed with his special recipe of the best dried Sockeye in the world. I loved all the activity of the harbor and an added benefit was that I could bring Jeffrey to work. Jeffrey and his Johnny Jump Up became regular fixtures at the office and he may have been the youngest legal assistant in the State of Alaska. Working for Mike added a layer of security, my husband's business was doing fine, we were building an addition to our home, and we were swaddled in mounds of baby blankets and bunting. It appeared we were building a life like any other young family, but we'd actually built a façade.

Ovarian cancer didn't take me and didn't claim my ovaries, but no matter how sweet the baby—the common thread that knit us together—there was a snag in our marriage that slowly unraveled the relationship we so desperately fought to keep intact. We had been working up to it for so long that when the last stitch came loose it was not a surprise.

Jeffrey was almost two years old and his parent's arguments were growing louder. Having no desire to fight in front of our child, Mike and I decided we should no longer live together. Mike popped the cork on a bottle of champagne he'd received from a friend and filled two glasses. We toasted our efforts and then calmly discussed divorce. Mike eloquently summed it up in ten little words: "Beck, we're just not two peas in a pod anymore."

Becalmed

In 1990, the day after St. Patrick's Day, Jeffrey and I left our little home on South Tongass and moved into an apartment. It was on the outdoor parking level floor of the Tongass Towers condominiums. I woke up every morning to the sickening smell of diesel exhaust fumes from the truck that parked under the broken window in my bedroom. The living room window was broken too and the floor covering was hideous brown and yellow shag carpet.

Jeffrey was extremely ill on our first night in the apartment and he christened the carpet with vomit that blended with the yellow shag. He often had ear infections requiring late night trips to the emergency room because his temperature was too high. As a new single parent, a blanket of calm warmed me as I administered pain and fever reducers to soothe my child. I felt reenergized and knew we would be all right.

Howls Echoing Off the Water

Mike issued a warning when I moved out. "Watch out for the wolves." Suddenly my phone was abuzz with strange low voices calling me at work to ask if I'd like to join them for dinner, lunch or movies. They didn't huff and puff around my apartment and besides a few strange encounters most of them extended Alaskan gallantry. But I hadn't taken out an ad in the daily news or purchased a 10-second sound bite on the radio to advertise my availability, and the attention was overwhelming.

Jeffrey and I took nightly walks downtown, dodging mud puddles and downspouts while singing *Rain Drops Keep Falling on My Head*. As I pulled him in his red wagon, men honked their horns and waved like lunatics. The attention was flattering and a nice boost to my self-esteem, but Jeff's daddy traveled these same few miles of road every day. The likelihood of him hearing the wolf whistles was high, and I wasn't comfortable with him witnessing such scenes. I was not divorced—just separated—and I had many issues to work out before I entered the dating realm. Mike and I may not have been living together but we loved each other and I had no desire for him to be hurt.

Back at the Helm

Broken windows, exhaust fumes, and rotten carpet didn't provide an ideal environment for Jeffrey and me and I was thrilled to find an apartment six miles south of town in the basement of a beautiful home. It had a lovely view and a nice play area for Jeffrey. Having to drive six miles back and forth to work seemed daunting, but the privacy of my new home was worth it.

I spent the next few months preparing to be officially divorced, reconciling being a single mom, and trying to figure out dating rules with Jody who I had been friends with ever since she showed up at my house to ask for a donation to the cancer society.

Ketchikan's new mall was still a novelty in town and when they announced the first annual Ball at the Mall—a formal event, almost unheard of in Ketchikan—women started shopping for dresses. Finally, there was a reason to be fancy and show off my starving new figure. Formal. I hadn't heard that word since my wedding. I tried on many variations of finery, and after many hours found the one.

A princess seamed, just above the knee, off the shoulder black velvet beauty. I had the dress and I had the shoes and I had the skinny little body to put into it, but I had forgotten one crucial element. I had no date.

The court date that would end my marriage to Mike was on the docket for the week after the ball. Surely, a public appearance with another man who'd caught my eye would no longer be taboo. It didn't take long before any flicker of that hope was doused.

The evening of the ball, I donned my dress and headed for Jody's house. I knew she would be able to help me with another small problem. I may have been wonderfully thin, but my bust line had diminished to two peas on a pale mannequin. She expertly stuffed my velvet bodice and sent me on my merry way.

My brother Mike took pity on his dateless sister and invited me to accompany him and his beautiful new girlfriend. I had never met Donna, and was not too excited to be the third wheel, but she and I hit it off immediately. Within a few years, she would become my sister-in-law.

My marriage officially ended in early December and I was in no mood for merriment or decorations. I selfishly refused to put up a tree. Luckily, my folks showed up with one for Jeffrey's sake.

On Christmas Eve morning, Jeffrey and I got up and I got ready to go to work. This was always a good day because Mike closed the office early. Ketchikan had just come out of a cold snap and the day was unseasonably warm. I strapped Jeffrey into the car seat and started the engine when I realized the car was idling on a sheet of water-covered ice. I stopped the car, set the brake, turned off the ignition, and stepped onto the driveway when the car started sliding down the hill. I grabbed the open driver's side door and tried to scramble into the driver's seat. My sleeve caught on something and I fell on my back as the car pulled me down the steep driveway, the tires threatening to flatten me into a cardboard cutout. Miraculously, the same gravel that ripped my coat stopped the car in the middle of the hill. I don't remember disentangling myself from the door, but I found myself standing on the neighbor's sidewalk screaming for my baby, who was snuggled in his car seat, oblivious to the drama. My right arm and backside looked like a bruised banana but other than that, I escaped unscathed.

I'd survived the year with all of its pitfalls, slippery slopes, and calamities. I started 1991 battered and bruised both physically and spiritually, but after months of being lonely I decided it was time to enjoy my life. I began dating but it was hard to be incognito with my ex-husband right down the road. Each date meant passing his house twice. Even though we were no longer married, we still cared for each other and dating was awkward.

I made a few mistakes in dating land. I had no idea how to simply have a good time. My suitors were interested in the fancy trimmings, the high heels, and the easy laughter. I let my guard down and had a few short-lived romances but soon learned they were only interested in the trappings but not the responsibilities. I quickly sifted men who were not interested in hearing about my little boy, or they dropped me on my head as soon as I started telling Mommy stories or scared them with ghost stories about cancer. There was nothing simple about my life and I needed more than flings or meaningless one-night stands. Three-year-old Jeffrey lent assistance in the minefield of men and mayhem. He made a bold announcement to a man I was flirting with in a restaurant, "you better not be thinking about marrying my mama!" If this didn't send them running nothing would.

Chapter 13

I decided to accept my fate and give up the quest for Mr. Right when my friends Aleta and Vic said they wanted me to meet some Teddy Bear of a guy nicknamed "Tippy," otherwise known as Rick Durkin. They thought we would be a great match, but after a few recent dating disasters, I was less than enthused. Aleta arranged an introduction for Thanksgiving. I stayed out all night the evening before with two friends and by the next morning I was exhausted, perhaps a bit hung over, and I thought I'd prove to the matchmakers what a colossal mistake they'd made. I arrived late and dispelled all promises of a fun, cute, friend. I hadn't washed my hair, bothered with makeup, or contributed any fixins to the meal. I refused to eat my vegetables and was uncharacteristically obnoxious. I did my best to ignore Tippy. He was very friendly and funny. He played with my friend's four excited children and contributed a lovely seafood casserole.

The next week a dozen yellow roses arrived at my office. The card said, "I would like to cook you a quiet dinner. No kids. No vegetables. I promise." I was still pouting about a short-lived flame, who hadn't bothered with flowers or goodies, so receiving such kind attention from someone I'd just met didn't thrill me. I called to decline the invite but I had a nasty cold and couldn't come up with an excuse fast enough. Besides, Jody said if I didn't accept the invitation she would. With the prompting of a trusted friend, I reluctantly accepted.

Fisherman's Feast

I arrived at Tippy's apartment late, not fashionably late, but rudely late. I walked right into the familiar apartment of one of

117

my recent failed romantic interests but the apartment was the only similarity. Tippy had obviously spent time planning a nice meal and was preparing a feast: chicken in a shrimp sauce, salad, homemade bread, and wine. Still reluctant to get my heart crushed again, I figured I'd bore him by talking about my son and my illness, all the while stuffing my cheeks with succulent shrimp. In between sneezes, I ignored my inner diet voice and gobbled down another piece of bread.

I talked for hours. My nose was so stuffed up I thought for sure Tippy was grossed out and ready to show me the door. Instead, he offered me a tissue and another glass of wine. I talked and sneezed and talked and sneezed until I was exhausted. He may have thought I was "opening up" but many a suitor had suffered through my stories. The difference was he seemed interested.

Months later he told me he called his mother after that first date and announced that he had found her. The girl he would marry.

We went on our second date a week later and decided to visit our mutual friends. It was winter dark when we left and as we walked towards the car, I stumbled into a deep gully at the edge of the property. Down I tumbled, finally coming to rest when my head collided with a sharp rock. Tippy had to turn on the car headlights to find me and help me climb out of the hole. He folded me into the car seat and when he got in the driver's side we both noticed an offensive odor. What I thought was the sulfuric smell from my journey to the center of the earth was actually the smell from the dog shit pit where I'd landed. I was wearing Tip's favorite black leather jacket, which instantly became mine. I was banged up and smelled awful. I should have cried but I laughed like a maniac and for some reason Tip thought I was adorable.

He came by a few nights later and shared a "Becky special" casserole *a la cheap ingredients* with Jeffrey and me. A week later he came by again, dug around in the fridge and helped himself to the week-old container of seconds. He was unaware of my typical diet dinner of Wheat Chex and about that time, it became evident that if we were to survive he would be in charge of meals.

Tip swiftly scuttled my reservations about our romance. A commercial seine fisherman for over a decade, he'd fished up and down the Alaskan coastline and enjoyed the life of a salty sailor. He'd snagged a few women in coastal towns but none of them were keepers. I was his prize catch and he was ready to drop anchor and live shoreside.

We had a whirlwind romance and by Christmas time Tip informed me he had designs on marrying me. I think the whole town accepted his proposal before I did. While I was out and about I kept hearing about my upcoming nuptials. Tip bought Jeffrey a huge pirate ship for Christmas. They played pirates for hours as the well-worn Peter Pan video played in the background. The man who liked my stories, and more importantly, loved my son, steadily began to infiltrate my heart.

Fond Farewell

Tip was a 100-ton license holder and he and Vic were hired to bring a yacht to Texas from Florida through the Intracoastal Waterway. He called me every time he was able to get to a phone to tell me of wild adventures through the bayou. We decided to take a trip to Hawaii when he returned and I couldn't wait. He was gone for a couple weeks and his answering machine was blinking urgently when he returned home. His mother had called several times and each message sounded more dire than the one before. She desperately needed to talk with him because his five-year old niece had been diagnosed with leukemia.

I met Tip's family in the worst of all possible scenarios. His mother Jane, her boyfriend, and his cousin Misty all met us at the hotel. Misty stared at me with beautiful blue eyes. She was in a wheelchair, and had not walked or talked since she was a toddler. Jane had adopted her and had been her loving caregiver for years. She showed such love for Misty, I knew she would be a wonderful mother-in-law.

The whole family went to the Ronald McDonald House to visit little Kristan and her parents John and Lynn. In the common areas, young bald children of all different shapes and sizes played with toys as their parents wiped away tears. Kristan had shiny waist length hair, but her skin was ashen and she was very ill. She was just beginning her battle with cancer and I was just beginning a new life. I felt an instant kinship. She loved dresses and so did I. Tip and I went out and bought her two "pretty pretty" dresses to cheer her up.

After we'd met the family, Tip and I flew to Hawaii for a week of subdued fun on the sandy beaches of Maui. During our stay we shopped in Lahaina, drove the winding road to Hana, swam the beaches, visited the Haleakala volcano summit, and enjoyed our honeymoon before the wedding. We spent an extra day in Seattle before returning to Ketchikan. Kristan was feeling better and we had a beautiful outing at the Woodland Park Zoo. She had a long road ahead full of chemo and sickness, and we all appreciated her smiles as we wheeled her around the park.

Tip moved in with me when we returned to Ketchikan. It seemed wise to have a trial run. I did not want to get involved in a relationship and find that it wasn't going to work. He extended an amiable hand to Jeff's dad and they both determined to get along, which was a relief for everyone, and they have been friends ever since.

Tying the Knot

I pictured a small private ceremony. I'd already had a large wedding and our combined household was overstuffed with toasters, coffee pots, and dishes. Tip and I didn't see the need for another large celebration, but I hadn't taken into account that his mom had waited a long time and a wedding was what she had in mind.

We were living on a tight budget so Rick found a beautiful suit at a second-hand store in Ketchikan when we were looking for a vacuum cleaner. The previous owner was probably deceased, which may seem a bit macabre, but Tip and I both have a caustic sense of humor. We splurged on a vibrant tie to complete the ensemble and a white tea-length dress with a fancy hat for me.

We married on October 17, 1992 in Longview, Washington—an easy commute for relatives from all over Western Washington.

Jeffrey and Kristan were the ring bearer and flower girl. Jeffrey wore a distinguished pewter colored suit with a pink bowtie, and he carried his favorite stuffed dog on the pillow. Kristan wore a brunette bobbed wig under a maroon felt hat and one of her "pretty pretty" dresses.

As the ceremony dragged on, Jeffrey lay down in front of the altar, rested his weary head on the ring-bearer pillow, and took a nap with the stuffed puppy. He jumped to attention just in time to approve of the nuptials and everyone snickered when the pastor tried to get me to vow to cook nightly meals. My old friend Tammie ended the ceremony with a lovely song and Tip topped off the celebration with a fresh Alaskan Salmon barbecue. Jeffrey played with his new cousins, Kristan and Danielle, and we enjoyed merriment with friends and family, many who were shocked that the single sailor had finally tied the knot and dropped anchor. The next day Tip, Jeffrey and I flew to Disneyland to mark the beginning of our magical adventure.

Chapter 14

By 1993 my cancer foe had been left for dead in the uterine trenches. Our small family enjoyed a charmed life in our blue 1930's home with its view of the Tongass Narrows. The bumblebee hum of floatplanes lifting to hover above the mountains, and the sound of the huge generators at the cold-storage plant woke us every morning. Our two-story shoebox had just enough room for the three of us and our slug eating German Schnauzer, Mandy. We settled in for a long winter, enjoyed a quiet Christmas, and looked forward to an exciting New Year.

Tippy and Jeffrey were thrilled when I announced a new baby was going to join the family. Within weeks it was evident this pregnancy would be nothing like the first. By four months, people started asking when I was due. I was convinced the baby should be born in August but my doctor argued for late September.

I tried to stay active but the baby kicked, roller-skated, and became a champion gymnast before it drew its first breath. By August I was unable to climb the rickety stairs to our dormer bedroom without having contractions, and even if I could, my awkward position made it difficult to maneuver out of our bed without whacking my head on the slanted ceiling. I was hospitalized twice for "premature" contractions that month. The stalling technique was an injection that made me a jittery, over-sized lunatic. I begged my obstetrician to let the labor proceed but she insisted the baby needed a few more weeks. I spent those last weeks languishing on a mattress in the middle of our microscopic living room, as the baby protested its September due date with relentless pummelings.

The house joined me in pregnancy and was ready to burst itself under the bloat of bassinets, bottles, and blankets. Mounds of trash bags overflowing with hand-me-downs surrounded my makeshift bedroom.

Every day after kindergarten Jeffrey asked, "Mommy have you had any more distractions?" I assured them there had been a few. Yes, this pregnancy had provided many *distractions*.

Jeffrey had been on his own for weeks, quietly playing with his toys, enjoying his captive audience. One day I heard him busily creating something in the kitchen, just around the corner from my makeshift bedroom.

"Don't worry, Mommy."

I'd learned that phrases starting with "nothing, Mom" or "don't worry, Mom" were usually cause for concern.

"What are you doing in there, Jeffrey?

"Making lunch."

"Didn't you eat at school?"

"This is for tomorrow."

I rolled myself off the mattress and carried my swollen belly into the kitchen. Jeff had opened up a jar of peanut butter, and his strawberry-blonde head was foraging in the fridge for a jar of jelly. I stood by as he glopped generous portions onto his bread. He cut the sandwich in half and placed one half each into a sandwich bag. He stuffed one of the halves into his lunchbox with some other goodies and placed it into the fridge alongside the other half-stuffed sandwich bag.

"See Mommy, now I always have a sandwich ready for the next day." We were all going to learn to be a few steps ahead and Jeffrey was instinctively preparing for the upheaval.

To add to the excitement, Tip was convinced our baby boy's name should be Bilbo. He was sure it was a boy and he wanted to bestow his child with the name of his favorite role model. I suggested name after name from the baby book but we could not reach consensus. He finally suggested we name the baby William, for my dad. The proper name would William Beauregard Durkin. It didn't take long to figure out what the nickname would be.

8.5 Pound Whopper

By late September, my obstetrician decided to induce labor because I was enormously overdone. On September 24, 1993, at four o'clock in the morning, on the day of the scheduled induction, I trudged down our front steps with the momentum of a steamroller as the baby planned an escape of its own volition.

The pain was frightening as my anxious baby plowed its way towards daylight with the force of a train barreling through a tunnel at top speed. I was angry when my doctor denied my laborious requests for pain meds since she'd had no difficulty with the labor stopping drugs or the planned induction treatment.

Fortunately, the non-induced labor was short lived and I forgot all about the tumultuous months of discomfort when a dark haired beauty with kissable lips rolled into the arms of her daddy.

Tippy invited Jeffrey and Mike into our celebratory room. While Mom and Jeff's dad and Tip huddled around the baby, Jeffrey sat on the edge of my hospital bed holding a precious bundle and sang, "Happy Birthday, Dear MacKenzie" to his baby sister for the first time.

MacKenzie's first act was to smack her dad in the face, knocking his contact lens clean out of his eye. We knew then this girl would be able to take care of herself. Her dad's swollen eye twinkled with pride.

Dad came by to visit his new granddaughter as often as he could before I went back to work. He nicknamed her Mazy and the rest of us called her MacKenzie Doodles. The name Doodles stuck for years and she completed our perfect family. I enjoyed a brief moment of time while MacKenzie satisfied my longing for all things pink, but she would indulge me for only so long. Fancy finery was not her forte, the fancier the finery the louder the shrieks. She shunned all outfits from the hand-me-down heap and any fashion-inspired creation that I set out. Finally, I capitulated and allowed her to be. She is simply MacKenzie, the best of her mom and dad: imaginative, beautiful, smart and sassy.

Parenthood—the remedy for couples everywhere trying to preserve their legacy. It doesn't come with the warning like they put inside the paper bag filled with the latest prescription. Nothing prepares one for the side effects of motherhood. One day you recognize your whole vocabulary is afflicted by baby talk as you share with great detail the latest amazing thing your child has done. As the children grow, so do the symptoms and gentle Jeffrey had not built up my immunities enough to deal with his younger sister.

Uncle Mike's day care was open for business again. I brought MacKenzie to work with me, but the law office day care arrangement was unsuccessful. Walks to the courthouse to show off a contented baby were not as I remembered and her screams echoed in the elevator. Unlike Jeffrey, whose favorite ride at Disneyland was the stroller, MacKenzie would have no part of the wheeled contraption. My docile boy did nothing to prepare me for my determined daughter.

Fishwife

I loved it when Tip's seine buddies came by for a visit. They were a friendly crew and I enjoyed the fishing jargon and spirited stories from seasons past. I was unprepared when one his crewmates announced he was going to captain a boat and was calling Tip on a sudsy promise to assist that he'd given over a few too many beers.

MacKenzie was less than nine months old when her dad, who would never renege on a fisherman's promise, packed his duffel bag for the Alaskan salmon season.

The boat was a dilapidated seiner that seemed destined for Davy Jones' Locker. Tip's primary engineering duty was making sure the five bilge pumps he installed kept the boat afloat. Sometimes he stood in three feet of slimy foamy fish water in the engine room trying to avert disaster. They were not able to fish the more lucrative Sockeye at Security Cove because the waterlogged vessel threatened peril every time the tender pumped the fish from the hold, and journeying too far could be perilous.

As my husband tried to keep a fishing boat a float, a rebellion was brewing on First Avenue. My mutinous children were upset about being abandoned and had turned into mischievous scalawags. Even the dog was misbehaving. My yard rebelled by shooting up weeds faster than I could pull them out. One lovely afternoon I came home to find Tammi and Spencer, Curt's wife and son, mowing and weeding my front yard. Sitting on the porch bench admiring the flowers and my finely trimmed lawn offered a little serenity to my otherwise stressed-out existence.

Being a fishwife was not my forte. I couldn't control MacKenzie, who was uncontrollable by day and inconsolable by night. The background laughter when Tip called ship to shore did not calm my tattered nerves. It sounded like he was enjoying a grand adventure while I drifted towards insanity.

I hung a white flag of surrender and Tip chartered a flight from the fishing grounds to right our listing family. The boat made little money that season, and Tip's excursion cost more than he earned.

After the fishing fiasco, we settled into a more stable and comfortable family life. I still worked full time for my brother and Tip worked various carpentry jobs. Our house was filled floor to ceiling with toddler toys and pirate booty. After our small German Schnauzer died, we added more chaos with a Chesapeake Bay retriever that took even more floor space. Jeffrey was happy in school and kept us entertained with his pirate wit. He made a Christmas scrapbook in school and his version of Santa's greeting was "Ho Ho Ho and a bottle of rum!" His wish for mankind was for a thousand vacuum cleaners to make the earth shine shine shine. He was a content little boy who was amused by his sister.

Kenzie never slept and she loved to climb and explore all the forbidden corners of our house. When she was about two we found her lying naked on top of a very high bookshelf. Another time we found her sitting on the inside lip of the fridge, sucking on a bottle of mustard. I was long past panicking over every episode—if I had, I wouldn't have survived her childhood—but I always had the camera ready to memorialize the wild child.

Listing Dangerously

Balance is a word Tip uses frequently. Yin and Yang. Good and bad. Profits and losses. His wonderful assets were balanced with financial liabilities. By virtue of matrimony, my neck became bound in the same IRS noose that had been cutting off his air supply for years. I came home one day to find a business card nailed to my front door. The bold print highlighted three dreaded words:

Internal Revenue Service.

The small card wielded such power. It signified oppressive and dire consequences and was heavy with the weight of Tip's debt. After recovering from the initial shock, I began the arduous task of convincing the government that I was not a slouch. I don't know what made Tip think they wouldn't catch up with him, and he refused to worry even though a federal anchor was hanging from his neck. His cavalier attitude worried me more than the threatening card.

1996 was already tinged with anxiety. As I bargained with the government to grant clemency to Tip, my brother negotiated with attorneys and clients over lawsuits. My brother Mike called me early one Saturday morning and asked me to come to work right away. He and Donna needed to fly south immediately to be with her mother, who was losing her battle with cancer. He didn't know when he would return.

The stress of dealing with the IRS and worrying about the office in Mike's absence loosened my fingers one digit at a time from the ledge I'd been desperately clinging to. I'd been wired and tired, unable to sleep, yet hardly awake for weeks. Certain I was headed for a heart attack, I gave in to the fear and took a trip to the ER where they performed an EKG and also drew some blood. The EKG was fine; I'd probably just suffered an anxiety attack. As an extra precaution

I was outfitted with a portable halter monitor to keep track of my heartbeat for about 24 hours. Round electrodes were affixed to my chest and wires peeked out from the top of my shirt. The monitor affirmed the EKGs findings. My ticker was ticking fine. Knowing I'd live to see another day, I dove back into pleadings and exhibit lists.

My blood work revealed my magnesium levels were extremely low because of my previous chemotherapy, which may have explained my over-anxious heart and fatigue. It also revealed an increase in my CA-125 levels (cancer antigen, tumor marker test). I had been getting the test for years since my original diagnosis and my levels were always under the not-to-exceed number of thirty-five. The elevated numbers were cause for concern. A week or so later I had my blood tested again and the CA levels were even higher. My nemesis, ovarian cancer, had silently crept into my life again.

I got the call at work. I pulled out my memo pad, donned my legal secretary hat, and began to jot down notes from my conversation with the nurse: CA levels rising. Oncologist contacted. Oophorectomy recommended immediately. Chemotherapy? Won't know until test results.

I don't remember crying or having any type of reaction. My heart was still. The panic ceased and I stoically crawled into an envelope of denial.

I drove out to Tip's construction site to tell him the news. A misty light drizzle beaded on my black wool coat while I explained the death of my figure was imminent. I was to have the dreaded surgery. The one his Grandmother foretold would make me get fat and go crazy.

Cancer was looming but it was too much to think about. I contacted my inner-Scarlet and fiddle dee dee'd myself away from the subject.

While I was coordinating my life with oncology offices I was told I might be eligible for a financial assistance program offered through a clinic affiliated with the hospital. I signed up for the program and was assured my visit would be complimentary. In return, I would offer my diseased organs for the benefit of medical students everywhere. The only catch was I would have to allow an intern to perform the surgery.

Once again, I made flight arrangements for travel to Seattle. I longed for a relaxed visit to the Emerald City, but instead of skipping my way through the streets of Seattle I was destined for a fortress, high atop Pill Hill, surrounded by a moat stocked with free radicals. I dusted off my gold card to the medical elite and extended the expiration date, hoping the need for it would expire before I did.

Jeffrey stayed in Ketchikan with his daddy and we brought Kenzie down to Olympia to stay with Tip's mom. When Tip and I arrived at the clinic in Seattle, we met the young doctor. She looked younger than me and I was amazed at her tiny hands—for some reason that struck me—maybe because she would be holding my life in them.

After the meeting, we went to the hospital for preliminary paperwork. This was when my careful planning fell apart. The financial office must not have received the memo about our arrangement with the clinic. The official-looking documents indicated we had too much income to meet the criteria for financial aid and they needed money before they would admit me to the hospital. I'd been leery of the too-good-to-be-true offer, but repeated assurances convinced me otherwise. I nervously clicked my pen while taking inventory of the office cubicle. Stapler, tape dispenser, paperweight; everything appeared normal though I felt anything but. Burning hives mottled my chest, and Tip's cheeks turned as crimson as Mike's had during my first chemotherapy treatment in Ketchikan.

The financial officer waited as I thumbed through my check register trying to determine if I had enough funds for a down payment on my surgery. This was not like a down on a house, car, or boat—something to be enjoyed—this was a down on my life. Whether I survived or not, the proceeds would live on in the jars that held my ovaries for macabre viewing and poking by med students. I pulled out my checkbook and scribbled out the payment. The amount was significant and left us completely broke. I only had the money because I had taken a second mortgage to pay down some bills including a settlement to the IRS. I wondered what would have happened if I hadn't been able to pay. Would I have been denied surgery? Sent out to the sidewalk to die?

Chapter 15

"Mommy, that lady has shiny red fingernails."

"Red fingernails are pretty, Jeffrey. Do you think I should use nail polish?"

Jeff giggled. "Silly Mommy. You're not of the *women's* age."

I looked at him quizzically. "What's the women's age, Jeff?"

"You know. *Older* ladies."

Jeffrey was seven-years old and Kenzie only two, but on February 28, 1996, I crossed an imaginary line from fertile young woman to a member of the "women's age" with a few nicks of the scalpel.

I checked into the hospital early in the morning and was instructed to don industrial-strength, anti-embolism stockings. They were so tight I was certain that in the course of preventing blood clots, they would stop all blood flow to my heart and I'd die anyway.

I began to obsess about everything from aspirating on the sip of water I swallowed when I woke up, to choking on a dab of tissue that stuck to my lip when I dabbed away the pre-op prohibited lipstick. You can't eat or drink before surgery and somehow I managed to break two cardinal rules before I even had my blood pressure checked.

I nervously attempted to joke around with Tip and his mom, but they weren't overly amused, and my mom looked drawn as she blinked back tears. I hadn't feared previous surgeries like I did this one. Maybe it was because of the kids. What would happen to my family if I died? What if this was it? I'd left Jeffrey with Mike but had not imparted any life-long wisdom or a letter he could hold forever. I'd left no instructions with his daddy about how to tell my little boy about his mother if she didn't come home. I'd forgotten to tell Tippy not to spoil MacKenzie too much and to remember to brush her hair every day, and that it wouldn't kill him to let my parents take the kids to Sunday School. How could I have forgotten to say a proper goodbye? My caustic sense of humor waned, and as I licked a tear off my upper lip, I knew I was a goner who had just committed her third no-eat-or-drink violation.

I was alone in a pre-op room and had plenty of time to work myself into a panic attack. I was sure I would have an adverse reaction to the anesthesia. When the nurses returned I tried to talk to them but it felt like someone had stuffed a roll of absorbent paper towels in my mouth. I choked out the words Jeff and Kenzie right before I was transported to the Land of the Ovary Snatchers.

I'd been in an anesthesia stupor as the ovary snatchers violated me. They dug into nodes, burrowed under organs, severed fallopian tubes, snipped my ovaries, and yanked out my uterus. Cancer had raped me once. The oopherectomy was no less sinister. Fastened by staples, I felt reduced to nothing more than a few reams of research for the medical archives.

The drab urology ward was the backdrop for my pasty pallor. Tip went to the gift store and bought me an afghan in mauve and blue tones to lighten the mood in my room. My family waited hours to learn the preliminary results of my cancer status, but no one arrived to give a hint about my prognosis.

Within hours of my surgery, a nurse came to my bedside and put a weird looking patch on my tummy, right next to all the bandages and staples. The patch was about 3" long by 2" wide and the consistency of a sandwich bag, but not nearly as attractive.

I whispered to Tip. "What is it?"

He shrugged his shoulders and looked at the nurse who was checking my pulse.

"It's a hormone patch," she said.

I adjusted my bed to the sitting position. "A what?"

"It's hormone replacement therapy—HRT. You're going to need it so you don't fall off the cliff."

I looked at Tip and shook my head in confusion. I didn't recall signing a waiver that warned me about a free fall towards middle age.

Bilious Tide

I was beginning to hate hospitals. I was nine years older, not such a cute patient, and the nurses weren't willing to jump at my every whim. Cancer was part of my patient profile, but I was not a twenty-four year old newlywed with my whole life in jeopardy. I was in a different demographic now. I still had life on the edge of peril, but the stakes weren't the same. There were no more cheery nurses to make me laugh or fix my makeup. I was Bed 2, Room 5.

Stark reality and nausea socked me in the gut. A bilious tide rose in my belly and as waves climbed higher a *helpful* nurse administered an antidote. As the nausea ebbed, another storm enveloped my entire body. A tingling in my toes climbed to my spine and crept up to my head. My hospital gown became a straightjacket and the IV tubing threatened to strangle me as I spiraled nearer the vortex.

Monitors, call lights, and flickering fluorescents added to my disorientation. Tip ran for the nurse, who determined I was having an adverse reaction, but there was no antidote for the antidote. I pleaded for my old friend, Morphine, but it wasn't as friendly as I'd hoped. As the panic slowly subsided, itchy hives took its place.

The nurses, vigilant in their pro-exercise routine, made me walk through the halls with my IV pole in tow. The lines kept getting tangled in my hospital wardrobe, designed for peepers and the less modest. As I did the IV shuffle, trailing well behind the un-fettered asses of the patients before me, I felt smug in the knowledge of the number one rule of the walk around the IV gauntlet: make sure your hospital gown is trussed-up well in the back.

I didn't have it in me to be a model patient anymore. Nurses darted in and out of my room but there was never a doctor in tow with test results. I felt unwelcome as I overextended my visit. I'd left my manners at the feet of my surgeon on the cold operating room floor, and Bounce-Back-Becky was nowhere to be found.

After several days of waiting, I finally learned my fate. No cancer detected. I had a "clean bill of health" and should expect to live a *normal* life. But my clean bill was the result of the enormous payment to purchase the health that had eluded me for years.

My doctor advised against traveling right away so Mom and I stayed in Seattle where I pondered a life of normalcy. Finally cleared for takeoff, I hobbled onto the plane in a bright purple leisure suit as familiar faces smiled at me from their assigned seats. My abdomen was wrapped in lumpy bandages and I had the gait of an old feeble woman. It was old home week on the Alaskan flight and a man who used to flirt with me when I'd been young and vibrant couldn't hide his shock as I tried to maneuver through the narrow plane aisle. In fear and pain, I bent over the tiny airline pillow, held my ears, and hummed my favorite psalm to keep the plane from falling out of the sky.

Back to the Shore

Three weeks after my surgery, Tip and I went to a party where all my friends saw me again for the first time. Doubled over and swollen, but doing my best to live my normal life, I smiled and sang songs from a comfortable perch on an overstuffed couch, but my party days were over.

I went back to work too soon after my surgery. Sitting for hours at my desk and climbing the hill to file pleadings at the courthouse was not conducive to my recovery. I decided to leave work early one afternoon and asked Dad to pick me up because it would be a few weeks before I was healed enough to drive. Dad and I were enjoying a leisurely lunch when I remembered –about two hours late—that Jeffrey's school had early release that day. Dad and I drove to the school but couldn't find my little boy. When we parked in front of my house, Jeffrey came running down the stairs of a neighbor's house, his cheeks red and blotchy and tear stung. Was Tip's grandmother right? I was already starting to feel crazy.

My brain was filled with fluff and I couldn't concentrate on anything. I didn't recognize the person in the mirror and I didn't like her much either. I didn't appreciate my misshapen tummy or the hormone patches that left adhesive marks all over my abdomen. The old and broken reflection couldn't possibly be me. I didn't have cancer but the girl looking back at me was unrecognizable and I considered death might have been an easier path.

Changing Course

The patch was no match for my hormone-starved body and they weren't kidding about falling off a cliff. I started having anxiety attacks about two months after my surgery. I'd drift into peaceful slumber only to wake up soaked in sweat with a bass drum pounding in my chest. I balled my pillow up and sat cross-legged in the middle of the bed, silently pleading for the noise to stop.

Daybreak was even worse. Kids crying, TV blaring, dogs barking, husband consoling, well-wishers calling, all contributed to the cacophony in my head. I picked up a laundry basket and flung it at a window. Shards exploded into the living room within inches of Jeff and Kenzie. Tip sent the kids to play in their room and tried to assure me it was okay—just an unfortunate accident. I knew the truth. I had broken through the chaos without considering the outcome. I had little control over my actions and even less on my emotions. The broken window cracked through Tip's beliefs that everything was okay in our gingerbread house on First Avenue. His wife was broken. I collapsed among the shattered fragments of what the window and I had become.

Prevailing over cancer was a badge of honor, but depression was a monster I was not equipped to fight. It hit fast and hard and was a sneaky opponent that pulled me into a dark hole and beat the shit out me. When it invited anxiety and panic to take their turns pummeling me, I cowered in the bottom of the pit unable to climb out, and no one heard my silent screams for help. I found solace in writing. I began to scribble crazy poems and stories on sticky notes and carried my green notebook everywhere I went.

Enter the Hormone War Zone

Hot Flash. Cold sweat. Change at thirty-five

A scorching hot reminder that I am still alive

Changes, changes, changes are happening to me

I wonder what it's all about

I wonder why me

The ovary snatchers had thrust me into Meno Meno Land. No survival kit accompanied my crash landing at the base of the Mount Hysteria, and I wandered desperately through a scorching hot valley. The volcano rumbled incessantly as I dodged lava streams and tried to deflect the molten rocks falling all about me.

I felt alone in the inferno. Sharing stories about cancer was easy. A twenty-something Alaskan woman in her first year of marriage, battling for her life, is a jaw-dropper in any crowd, but discussing menopause with friends who were still young and vibrant left me cold.

I could no longer concentrate on their chatter, I was too busy waving down the waitress who'd been remiss in refilling my glass of ice water—the cool condensation-clad container that doubled as a freeze pop to roll on my neck. My relaxed friends didn't seem to notice. As they were chilling out, I was melting into menopausal mush. They had time to ease into "The Change" to prepare, to change eating habits, to exercise. They were on a gradual descent into the heat, while I'd been plunged into the inferno. I'd crash-landed in six hours flat.

Other than cancer, my ovaries had never given me any grief. It is only the absence of them that had me yearning for the keys to the body parts room where I imagined them floating like buoyant eggs in a canning jar. I longed for them—especially at night—when a warm tingling in my cheeks rapidly moved to my neck and I found myself in hell dodging fireballs. Impaled on a rotisserie, rolling round and round in my bed, my once cool sheets threatened to suffocate me until a gust from the ever-present fan hit condensation beads on my skin and plunged me into an arctic freeze.

My outfits consisted of loose sweat pants, a tank top, and a polar fleece jacket. My beverage of choice rotated between ice-cold water and jitter-laced coffee. All thoughts of social interaction were peppered with panic; was there a chilly escape route?

It was hard to remember a life beyond cancers borders, where once upon a time I was a normal girl whose fairytale enemies bore benign sticks and stones. But my fairytale ending had been rewritten.

The twenty-three year old baldheaded woman turned her blazing blue eyes to face the malevolent cancer dragon. She consumed mystical potions concocted to shrivel the creature, and her two children—born in defiance of the monster—forced it to recoil back into its lair.

Several years later, her ovaries were wrenched from the malignant clutches of the cancerous beast, but as she smote the dragon it exacted vengeance, huffing and puffing its final death flame—a scorching menopausal heat—licking the back of her neck for eternity.

My doctor eventually pulled the patch and prescribed a little green pill consisting of conjugated equine estrogens called Premarin—Pregnant Mare Urine. I wondered if things could get any worse. I'd lost my reproductive organs and replaced them with horse pee to trick my brain into thinking I was still vital.

Chapter 16

I prevailed over cancer but we never fully recovered from the surgical and financial impacts of my hysterectomy. Tip was always sniffing the employment trail, and the highs and lows of my attitude correlated with the highs and lows of his employment. I had been working at my brother's law office for years. Longevity was my middle name. Tip may have retired his post on seine fishing boats, but he still lived in seasonal mode. He had years of life in cycles; summer fishing in Alaska, winters in Mexico. Settling down for him meant feet on the shore—the equivalent of hibernation. When he couldn't find work he baked. Homespun concoctions wafted from the kitchen. One day I came home from work to find the counter overflowing with Key Lime pies. My rebellious body jumped into those like a swimmer going for the gold. An unemployed husband, a bakery bill, and a zillion calories became my reality.

Tip worked on some great carpentry jobs. They paid well and he enjoyed them. Unfortunately, carpentry was calamitous. Just a few days into a job he slipped on an icy plank and broke his foot. Another time he was working on a church when I got news that I should meet him in the emergency room. I found him lying on his back with a 3.5 inch, barbed, 16-penny nail pinning his shirt to his side. He'd fallen off a ladder and on the way down caught the trigger of his nail gun. The X-Ray revealed the nail sitting just above his hipbone. Somehow he'd avoided all major organs. The ER doc decided against surgery and came to Tip's bedside with a large pair of pliers. He put one leg on the side of the bed for leverage and with maximum torque pulled the barbed nail out of Tip's flesh with a thwack. Next came a shot of antibiotics into the wound and they sent him on his way.

Another time he was working on a roof for a friend when the man accidentally shot him with the nail gun, this time pinning his overall strap into his shoulder flesh. Nail riddled flesh and broken bones turned our home into a horror movie set.

Fishing for Jobs

Tip also skippered charter boats for summer tourists. He'd spent so much time as a chief engineer or first mate on boats, where each crewmember had their tasks, that skippering charter boats was not an easy transition. Paying customers were not crew and he didn't find their whining about not limiting out on salmon endearing. The cruise industry touted Ketchikan as The Salmon Capitol of the World. The tourists expected to deckload the pleasure craft with fifty-pound whoppers. They wanted bragging rights and photo ops. Fishing being fishing—it was common to return to port with nothing more than wet shoes and the sniffles. Tourists who'd parted with a few bucks could be venomous if they didn't catch a fish. One woman raised such a ruckus Tip had to confine her to the cabin. Rather than a gratuity, he had to answer to a scathing review for his tyrannical tactics.

Chugging Down the Channel

In the spring of 1997, Tip found the perfect job as First Mate on a tugboat. He left one day in March and didn't come home until October. The kids weren't such a handful by then and I dealt with his absence much better than the last time, but I could never sleep when he was gone. Either Kenzie kept me awake or I was afraid that each creak or groan from our old house was the bogeyman waiting to pounce.

I loved the sound of Tip's happy voice when he called me from the helm during late night relief-captain duties. He and the captain had all kinds of adventures at sea and they loved to call and tell us about them. Jeffrey and Tip swapped pirate stories, and MacKenzie made sure Tip was taking care of the ditty bag she'd packed for him containing stuffed animals to keep him company. The captain in the background saying, "take 'er back to Dora" or "take 'er back to

Dolomi" meant more logs to be barged from Dolomi's helicopter logging operation to the sorting yard in Dora Bay, which translated to more money in the Durkin bank account.

Being separated wasn't easy but sometimes I took time to write down my thoughts. I wrote this poem one evening while I was missing Tip:

My Husband, Their Mate

He's out to sea
it's been calling him for years
this time I'll let him go
without so many tears

The salt and the water are in his blood
it cannot be denied
to master the sea with all its force
fills his soul with pride

I said a "fishwife" was not for me
I won't lose my husband to the sea
Those words I said not long ago
but the sea called again and I couldn't say no

So with a kiss and a gentle hug
off he goes he's first mate on a tug

And though it's hard to sit here alone

seafaring men are a breed of their own

It's why I'm drawn to men of the sea
to their special bond and camaraderie

From ship to shore you can hear his pride
the crew in the background know he's speaking with his bride

The times that he's home
with feet on the shore
I've learned to treasure
because the sea won't be ignored

Dedicated and true to his fate
he is First Mate on the Chatham Strait

He'll leave once again
with kisses and hugs
and walk down the ramp
he's first mate on a tug

I wrote the poem thinking it was a silly little ditty, but MacKenzie clung to the words and it became her bedtime story. Tears dripped onto the page as she recited the last stanza.

Another thing that helped our bank account is that Tip, the condiment king, was not home to wander his favorite aisle of the grocery store. Our fridge was often empty of food, but we had toppings for every imaginable delicacy. Chutneys, mint jelly, marmalades, curries, and exotic butters filled the shelves, and he could prepare a meal out of toppings alone, but my culinary skills had been scuttled along with my Easy Bake Sewing Machine. When we lost our cook to the tugboat galley, I was so intimidated by the condiments he'd left behind, the kids and I took solace at the drive-up window.

Tip bought me a plane ticket that year so I could spend my birthday with him on the tug. After living in Alaska for over twenty years, I was finally going for a floatplane ride, but my flying fears had worsened with each flight south for surgeries. My anxiety meter rose as I walked down the ramp and gingerly stepped onto a pontoon. The pilot gave me headphones and had me sit in a front seat so I could enjoy the sights and not get airsick. My hands were shaking and I knew at any moment I might freak out and try to jump out of the plane. We taxied into the Tongass Narrows just as I'd witnessed thousands of times from the window at my brother's office. The plane lifted off easily but I was terrified when after just a few seconds in the air we started back down towards the water. The pilot hadn't mentioned we would be stopping at the airport on Gravina Island to pick up a few more people and the quick descent was frightening.

We bumped along on choppy water for our second takeoff and this time we flew high over hidden lakes and mountains. It was an unseasonably hot and clear day and as the plane buzzed along like a bloated bumblebee, it looked like I could have reached out and touched the treetops.

The plane set down lightly on the smooth water at Dolomi, an old gold mine camp turned logging camp on Prince of Wales Island. The captain helped me hop off the pontoon and into the skiff and then he ferried me to the tugboat. Tip had a big double-bunk cabin all to himself in front of the noisy engine room. It was full of all the comforts of home—favorite books, TV, paintings, pictures of the kids, Kenzie's stuffed animals and the poem I'd sent him.

I'd landed in a remote area of Southeast Alaska where there was active logging going on. After Tip introduced me to the crew, I found a seat by the smokestack and watched the crane operator skillfully pile logs onto a barge. When the barge was full, we chugged out of the inlet and headed to the sorting yard in Dora Bay. Later that night I watched Tip run around in cork boots hopping from log to log on open water. A flashlight in his mouth and starry skies above illuminated his precarious path as he secured rafts, which seemed like a tooth-breaking, choking hazard to me. The next day a large wave washed over the bow, catching a deckhand unaware. The wave struck him with such force his bridgework came loose and lodged in his throat. Tip administered the Heimlich maneuver, saving the man the indignity of choking on his own teeth, which assured me he could probably save himself if he choked on his flashlight.

The captain and crew took good care of me as I lounged on the red deck and soaked up the sun. I caught my first Sockeye salmon from the stern of the tug as a black bear cooled off in a stream during the record-breaking heat. The crew set up a deck barbecue and the smells of cedar and spruce mingled with hydraulic and engine oil fumes, adding to the aroma of my sizzling Sockeye.

Though I was thrilled to finally experience what so many Alaskans take for granted I couldn't be persuaded to hop back on the floatplane that had delivered groceries to Dora Bay. I extended my visit by several hours due to my chauffeured tugboat ride back to Ketchikan.

Ship to Shore

Even with Tip gone, our darling house on First Avenue did not provide ample accommodations for our family and our new rambunctious puppy. We tripped over each other just walking through the living room. Extra money, loneliness and boredom, brewed a concoction of house hunting frenzy not alleviated until I signed on the dotted line. I found the perfect house about 16 miles from town—a world away if you live in Ketchikan. It wasn't easy to obtain original signatures from Tip as he was floating around Southeast Alaska. Due to a wicked storm, he'd been out of cell range for over a week and I hadn't been able to coordinate where to fly the loan documents. They'd anchored up to wait out the storm, and Tip couldn't believe I'd managed to pinpoint the tug's location. I got ahold of a caretaker at a mothballed logging camp on Long Island and sweet-talked him into taking the documents out to the tugboat, waiting for Tip to sign them, and putting them on the next plane back to town.

We found room for all our stuff in our new three-story house when we took possession that fall. The kids had their own space, Jeffrey didn't have to share his room with the washer and dryer, and Kenzie's room was set up with an easel for painting pictures to send to her daddy. Tip had a huge shop and double garage to tinker in when he wasn't at sea, and I appreciated being able to sit straight up in bed without hitting my head on the dormers. And so far I hadn't had to wave a white flag of surrender as I watched Tip chug on by from my bedroom balcony.

We had a ship to shore radio rigged up, which was more economical than our cell phone, but not conducive to private conversation. It was fun to talk on the radio and I enjoyed hearing the operation from afar. Unfortunately, the radio could also share bad news or hint at a non-salvageable relationship. The conversations from my kitchen barstool to the tug's wheelhouse were lighthearted and mushy in comparison.

Whirlpool to the Bottom

Tip worked non-stop for several months and when he wasn't at sea he was on call. It was always hard to see him go, but I had never seen him as happy as when he walked down the ramp with dozens of donuts for the crew. In March of 1998 the predictable and completely inconvenient calls we had learned to expect from the captain grew fewer and farther apart. Tip maintained his on-call status until June of 1998 when our livelihood began to list dangerously. We were devastated when his life as First Mate went up in the same smoke of the imploded pulp mill. He once again dropped anchor and attempted to regain his land legs.

He picked up odd carpentry jobs and we eked out a meager existence, but not enough to pay the mortgage on the house we had just made comfortable for our little family. A business partner decision with another carpenter made things even worse. The partners dreamt of a successful business, but a process server bearing the documents of our demise interrupted their dreams. We became victims of circumstances no one could have ever foreseen.

Cancer seemed controlled and I'd humbled the panic attacks, but now a malicious troll threatened my sanity. Financial difficulties, humiliation over defending a lawsuit, and danger of losing our house created an inconsolable wrinkle in my not-so-neatly pressed life.

Depression and anxiety grabbed hold with a grip so tight I had a constant headache. I desperately tried to uphold my protective visage, but fatigue pulled on every pore. I no longer felt comfortable in my Ketchikan cocoon. My once familiar stomping grounds seemed like foreign soil. The lightness in my high-heeled step as I made my daily walk to the courthouse slowed to a clumsy traipse in hideous loafers. I hid behind oversized clothes and my black coat became a shroud as I shuffled through Ketchikan's tunnel—the dark umbrella that shielded me from the elements for almost thirty years. Stepping into the courthouse elevator was fraught with anxiety over meeting an attorney from the opposing party. I no longer lingered to chat with court clerks or jest with judges. Once more I'd abandoned my bounce-back-ability and mumbled "get lost" when folks I used to greet on the street said I'd be prettier if I smiled.

I set my electric blanket to permanent high, eager to abandon my family and enter dream world. But there was no relief in sleep. Within minutes of closing my eyes, demons hurled bricks at my chest and sucked the air out of my lungs. Sitting upright and rocking over my pillow, I willed myself to crawl away from the panic, but it was attached to me and followed me everywhere. I resented Tip snoozing beside me, but he was powerless to deflect the invisible bricks.

In a brief moment of sanity, I called a psychiatrist.

Diagnosis: Major Depression.

No surprise there. It definitely didn't feel like a minor case. The shrink bandied about the names of a full medicine cabinet's worth of curative potions: Prozac, Trazadone, Zoloft, Zanax.

Rx: take it slow, build up a tolerance, expect great results within weeks, return in one month. Apparently, in addition to depression and panic attacks I was also suffering a bit of paranoia, which made it difficult to pop the powerful pill. I waited days before swigging my first knock-me-on-my-ass dose of Trazadone. Immediately after I set down the glass, I counted every pill in the bottle at least five times because I knew I had inadvertently swallowed more than the recommended dosage and would never wake up. This flung me into the worst panic attack ever as Tip shook his head cursing the unseen enemy claiming his wife, before I fell into a medicinal stupor.

The Trazodone was miraculous. I slept like Rebecca Van Winkle.

Because of my love for the drug, I had to cold turkey myself away from the cure. My doctor switched my meds and allowed me to gobble Prozac. In a matter of weeks my psyche was significantly improved. Wrapped in artificial happiness, the pill worked so well I no longer needed the comforting tunes I constantly hummed. I stopped writing poetry. I didn't need food. I didn't need people. Someone could have died and I wouldn't have cared. I seemed to be feeling optimistic, but I was actually void of any feelings at all. With the ingestion of Prozac I became a literal numbskull. A Prozac Polly smile was glued on my lips, as my hips and tummy grew to amazing proportions, an unplanned for side effect of the happy pill. And for the first time in my life, fat didn't seem so bad as my chubby cheeks accompanied my equally expanded bubble-butt.

At some point, I began to wonder about my overblown attitude of optimism as my thigh-chaffing waddle threatened to split the seams in my jeans. The pills were trying to fool me. There was no evidence my new obese body was a good thing, and clearly I had things to be upset about. I didn't feel that prior to the happy pills I'd been out of touch with reality, either cynical or pessimistic. I determined my life had been fairly shitty of late and that I had been feeling anger, sadness and betrayal because I had finally dropped the plastered mask of one in deep denial. My mask was so stretched after years of use and abuse that when the seams finally cracked, everything I had been suppressing from my cancer days, hysterectomy, financial woes, and legal problems came forth and punched me in the gut.

My shrink suggested when I was ready I ought to contact my inner child. I had no desire for that conversation. I had safely tucked her into a file cabinet in the back drawers of my brain. I called on her only to reflect on happier times. Bad memories, whatever they may be, needed to remain buried.

Chapter 17

We had fantasized about leaving Ketchikan for years and it was fun to dream. Dreams don't need to be grounded in reality. Moving was not best for Jeff and the decision to leave was agonizing. Tip was familiar with life on the outside, but it was unimaginable to me. Ketchikan offered a craggy security. It was not always easy, but I knew it well. It operated at an unhurried pace where the top speed limit was 55 mph. I couldn't imagine leaving my home and family, all my friends, and my Forever Cheechako life.

I wrote my letter of resignation several times before placing it in the wall pocket at my brother's law office. I'd worked with him for eleven years and we enjoyed a special bond. Being over the water brought marine life right under the office where critters hid at low tide. Where else was I going to turn towards an open office door to find an otter who had wandered in for legal advice?

I would miss my huge picture window above the Tongass Narrows where Tip first spied me after paddling over from Vic and Aleta's place on Pennock Island, prior to our fateful Thanksgiving meeting. And where every morning I watched the bow of my brother's skiff as it rounded the north end of Pennock Island, and then at full throttle ride bouncy waves across the Narrows, indicating that it was time to put on a fresh pot of coffee. I was doing more than simply quitting a job; I was leaving my brother.

The news of the impending move was difficult for my folks. Five-year-old Kenzie told Mom, "Gramcracker, you've had me for my whole life. It's time for you to share me with Grandma Jane." Of course this didn't stop the tears from flowing down my parent's cheeks as their only daughter told wild tales of moving away into the great Washington abyss, just as Curt, Tammi, and Spencer had done a few years before. They could not reconcile a life on the rock without their grandchildren. Worries ensued over what to do with Jeffrey. We agreed to take him to Washington for the summer, return him to finish sixth grade, and then have him start junior high with us.

Leaving on a Minus Tide

The pills were my escort off the rock where I had spent the last twenty-seven years, which was similar to escaping Alcatraz. They are both on a rock. They both imprison. Each one requires stamina to survive and life on the outside feels like life-long probation. You never know when it will call you back. The same things that imprisoned, also offered comfort. We knew our neighbors—good, bad, or indifferent. We were part of the seascape, yet unique in our Alaskan ways. Because we were all island dwellers, the playing field was evenly scored: lawyers, doctors, and bankers all broke bread with loggers, fishermen, and bush pilots. I left fellow prisoners on the rock. I left the only life I knew. I left with the knowledge that I might spend several agonizing years separated from Jeffrey, my island boy.

We held a giant garage sale reminiscent of one so many years ago when my family left Whidbey Island. People rummaged our belongings but this time I had a say in what was loaded in the moving van. Tippy left a week earlier with our two Australian Cattle dogs, Lloyd and Linda, and our ferocious Siamese cat.

Ebb and Flow

We rented a small house at Agate Beach, several miles out of downtown Shelton, Washington, where we enjoyed a delicious anonymity in the idyllic setting. Our neighbors didn't know us. We had no history. No one knew about my cancer, the lawsuit, my mental anguish. We had apple, fig and walnut trees, and succulent berries. I got busy making luscious desserts and fantasizing about becoming the best June Cleaver mom ever. Lloyd and Linda retrieved sticks from the cove and swam around the kids and me in the chilly water. Our first summer was sweltering with very little rain, and I insensitively bragged to my Alaskan friends that the only time I turned on the windshield wipers was to wipe away the dust. I learned about the importance of sunscreen when my waterlogged skin erupted in freckles. Tip was happily building houses for a local contractor, while his housewife—in an unprecedented move—greeted him at the door with home-cooked meals.

Everything was wonderful until Jeffrey's end-of-the-season return to Alaska. He entered his airline confirmation code into a computer kiosk and handed a summer's worth of luggage to the agent with her sticky smile. I stood by in case I was needed, but I wasn't. Jeff had the routine down. Punch a number. Print a pass. Leave his family. While I sat stoic in a row of connected chairs, trying to ignore the strangers surrounding me, I concentrated on how much I hated the airline for taking my boy away to Alaska.

We waved goodbye as Jeff weaved through the maze of the security area. The line snaked closer to the gate as Jeff passed from the security of his mama to the security guard waving his wand. Where was my wand? Why couldn't I wave one to freeze the moment and bring Jeff back?

The ebb and flow of the tides echoed the ebb and flow of our lives. My whole existence revolved around my son's return back to Agate Beach, but Jeffrey was at home on Bugge Beach in Ketchikan. Friends and laughter and bon fires filled his happy days while I stared out my window awaiting an imaginary ship containing my precious cargo.

Adrift

Packing our bags and moving to Washington with the realization that Jeffrey would have to divide his time between two distant shores was heavier than any millstone. While the panic attacks ensued, I felt that stone as it pulled me under. My soft blue sheets became whirlpools sucking me to dark and treacherous depths. And it was under that I wanted to stay. But morning brought Kenzie to my bedside singing *Shoo Fly Don't Bother Me* to lessen my pain. Shamed into submission, I dragged my ass out of bed, showered all the salty tears from a sleepless night, and watched them trickle down the drain. No sleight of hand or makeup could diminish my puffy veined eyelids. I'd aged a year overnight.

It took a long time to become acclimated to Washington. Tip and I experienced a series of U-turns, Caution signs, and Dead Ends. One of us would settle into a promising position at work and the other one would lose their job. The only constant in our life was constant change.

The ripple effects of the implosion of Ketchikan's pulp mill followed us to Washington when yet another job site was demolished. This time an assisted living facility where he was a maintenance director was razed in favor of a parking lot, displacing both residents and workers. Once again, our livelihood was threatened.

The kids were more resilient and routine beget normalcy. Mandatory schooling set their path, though Jeffrey was not too happy about his dual citizenship between two shores. Kenzie loved school and kept us entertained with her antics. A crafty kindergartner, she once made the whole household late when she changed every clock for April Fool's Day.

For many years, I maintained a dual personality: the public persona with the easy smile and infectious laughter, kind, easy-going, and compassionate. Then there was the other girl who only came out at night. She waited until the kids and Tip were asleep and then let her dogs snuggle in beside her to lap up her tears.

I gave up on sleep. It was hard enough to be awake, but sleep brought its own terror and nightmares. During a routine doctor appointment to get a lab slip for my yearly cancer antigen test, I mentioned insomnia to a doctor who summed up my ailment in two words: stress and depression. Again. As she pulled out her prescription pad, I explained that under the circumstances I felt it normal to be depressed and that I didn't want to take more pills. She handed me the sheet and assured me the pills would help.

My cancer antigen was fine, and considering I'd dodged cancer again, I had serious reservations about the need for a new pill, but the latest concoction had the added benefit of anorexia. Hmmm, weight loss and sleep vs. panic attacks and obesity. She got me. She waved a self-esteem cure in front of my bruised and battered spirit. I took the bait and lost the weight. A few months later I'd lost about twenty pounds along with my sanity. The new miracle drug caused fuzzy brain and severe stomach pain, which raised red flags and an order for a CT Scan. I had come full circle. I was treated for depression and anxiety, ended up with tummy ache, was shoved into the CT tunnel of doom to see if the cancer had returned—all because of a pill that was supposed to make me feel better.

Pop a pill, never heal. If pills really mended broken hearts, why was I so sad? If pills really conquered anxiety why was I still anxious and unable to sleep? I'm not saying they didn't have their uses and I'm glad that medicines were available to me, but my suffering had grown resistant, immune to the pill's curative powers. I needed more than denial Novocain for my brain. Denial of the cancer had been a useful tool when I was first diagnosed—a shield against realities I couldn't face, but at some point I needed to face my enemy. Fight for my sanity. Kick the shit out of the anxiety demons and move forward. After a tense argument between my husband and my doctor I tossed the mind numbing, pain producing pills. My stomach stopped hurting and my brain eventually cleared enough to start dealing with reality.

When I was asked to submit a story for inclusion in a book called *Suffer the Women* my anguish bubbled to the surface. The premise of the story was supposed to be based on my bout with ovarian cancer, but mid-way through the writing my fingers tapped out a different tale. The abyss for me was never about the cancer, the convenient illness used to hide deeper issues. The deep dark hole that held me was a self-inflicted exile for abandoning my son. My mantra, *I will not accept the unacceptable* was an armored shield against anyone who tried to penetrate my self-loathing. Forgive myself? Never. The *Suffer the Women* project stripped my feelings bare. Finally acknowledging them was the first step towards stretching beyond and moving towards healing.

Return to Navigable Waters

Anxiety demons still knock on my bedroom door occasionally, always waiting until everyone else is in deep slumber, but they are not allowed residency. They still try to hurl their bricks at my chest but I'm armed with coping mechanisms. My new favorite mantra: *I choose to be happy, I choose to be happy*, has them unable to get a firm grip.

My battle with cancer made me strong. It taught me to take nothing for granted. To let those I care about know I love them. To always be honest, and even if I find some things unacceptable there are just some things I cannot control.

My life hasn't always been easy, but it is interesting. A trip to the doctor is always validation when they raise their eyebrows, set down their laptops, and ask me to explain how I was diagnosed with ovarian cancer in 1985, had two children after that, and did not have my ovaries removed until almost ten years later. I laughingly tell them it's a long story.

They tell me I'm fortunate. I could argue that fortune would have been the avoidance of cancer and calamity, but what I lost on the operating table has been returned in ways I would never have expected. I don't long for unattainable things. I don't think I need to be wealthy to be successful. I'm satisfied with precious moments. I don't mind when it rains. I'm happiest when I'm talking with my kids, riding bikes with Tip, writing stories, visiting with friends and family, and playing with my pups. I'm especially happy my parents no longer need to worry about their fragile daughter.

A bi-product of a terrible illness and the subsequent fallout is being able to comfort and empathize with others who may be at the beginning of an arduous journey. Without the trials, I never would have experienced the joy of sharing and to honestly say "I understand."

My children are both adults now. Jeffrey recently bought a house, and Kenzie graduated from junior college. This week I will celebrate my 53rd birthday with my family.

I'm no longer hiding behind my smiles. I'm smiling because I'm happy.

THE FACTS

Ovarian cancer is one of the five leading causes of cancer related death in American women.

A woman's lifetime risk is 1 in 72.

Each year, almost 22,000 women are diagnosed and about 14,000 women die of ovarian cancer.

A woman's chance of survival is better if the cancer is found early.

A Pap test does NOT detect ovarian cancer, it tests for cervical cancer.

WHAT SHOULD I LOOK FOR?

Ovarian cancer has symptoms. Take action and see your doctor, preferably a gynecologist, if the following symptoms are unusual for you and occur 12 or more days in a given month:

- Bloating
- Pelvic or abdominal pain
- Difficulty eating or feeling full quickly
- Urinary symptoms (urgency or frequency)

Additional symptoms have been commonly reported by women with ovarian cancer. They include fatigue, indigestion, back pain, pain with intercourse, constipation and menstrual irregularities. These symptoms are not as useful in identifying ovarian cancer because they are also found as often in women who do not have the disease.

Ovarian Cancer
NATIONAL ALLIANCE
We Work To Save Women's Lives

(202) 331-1332 www.ovariancancer.org

WHO GETS OVARIAN CANCER?

All women are at risk for ovarian cancer, but some are at higher risk:
- Women with a family or personal history of ovarian, breast or colon cancer
- Post-menopausal women
- Women who have never been pregnant or given birth

WHAT CAN REDUCE THE RISK OF OVARIAN CANCER?

- Oral contraceptives
- Pregnancy and breast feeding
- Tubal ligation/hysterectomy
- Removal of the ovaries and fallopian tubes

WHAT CAN YOU DO TO DETECT IT?

Until a screening test is found:
- Have your yearly well-woman visit.
- If a family member has cancer, discuss regular monitoring with your doctor.
- If you have symptoms, ask for a pelvic exam, transvaginal ultrasound and a CA-125 blood test.
- If ovarian cancer is suspected, consult a gynecologic oncologist. To find one in your area, call the Foundation for Women's Cancer at 1-800-444-4441.

FOR MORE INFORMATION VISIT
WWW.OVARIANCANCER.ORG
OR CALL (202) 331-1332

too delicate to manage more than a magnum or two. Surely your guests require more than that. No, I insist, Majesty. Let me be of service." He took my arm.

I felt trapped. I was furious inside at the Cardinal's presence spoiling my amorous opportunity with Axel. But I also felt helpless in the face of his cunning and forcefulness.

My mind raced as we walked on towards the Petit Trianon. I was reasonably sure that Axel had followed me, but if he had, and he saw me with the Cardinal, he would probably not presume to approach us. *Merde!* Were others always to thwart our joining?

"What did you say?" My ruminations had blurred the Cardinal's words.

"I was inquiring about the diamond necklace."

The Cardinal knew that he did not have to be any more specific than that. There was only one diamond necklace. It was that one assembled by the jewelers Bohmer and Bassenge for Mme. Du Barry. Their quest for flawless gems had taken years and the necklace itself had only recently been completed. With Du Barry out of the picture, they had shown it to me and I had fallen in love with it. There was only one problem: the price.

The jewelers were asking the incredible sum of 1,600,000 livres for the necklace. Even King Louis' supply-side economics could not support such a purchase. For the first time in our marriage, Louis had refused to buy me something I wanted. His decision was final, and so I had resigned myself to doing without it.

"Nothing has changed," I told the Cardinal with a sigh. "The diamond necklace will never grace my bosom."

"It is the luster of the necklace which will suffer," he assured me smoothly.

"You haven't changed." I chuckled in spite of myself. "You still turn a wicked compliment."

was mine. I made it a point never to invite him to my soirées at the Petit Trianon or to my gambling parties. In effect, as queen I successfully excluded him from the social life of the Court.

For a man who savored court intrigues—both political and erotic—as much as Cardinal Rohan always had, such an exclusion was a bitter pill. As cardinal he kept apartments at Versailles of course, and had the freedom of the grounds, but my *intime* gatherings were private and off limits to him. Because this was understood, I was both surprised and outraged to encounter him now.

"How come you here, sir?" I greeted him coldly.

"I am taking the night air, Majesty." His blue eyes were intense. The silver tipping his straight black hair at the temples glittered in the moonlight.

"You are intruding on private festivities!"

"I apologize, Majesty. It was not intentional. I have only chosen to walk in the gardens at what would seem to be an inopportune moment. But your party is not in the gardens, Majesty. Is it?"

I sensed that he was mocking me. Had he guessed that an assignation was involved? If he became privy to such an indiscretion, he would not hesitate to use such knowledge against the King, and against me as well if it was to his interest. I must not let my scorn of him outweigh my self-interest. With this thought, I tempered my attitude.

"No," I answered him, my tone more conciliatory. "My party is not in the gardens. It is just that we have run out of champagne and I am on my way to the Petit Trianon to fetch some more."

"I will help you carry it, Majesty?" He raised a wicked eyebrow.

"I don't need any help. I can manage."

"But how, Majesty?" He spread his hands. "You are

be alone with my strong young Swede was the real reason.

A thrill coursed through me when a man's figure appeared on the path. At first the moonlight was in my eyes and I could only make out its outline. The figure was tall and handsomely built. But I saw as I drew closer that it was dark-haired and mature, rather than blond and youthful. The visage was French, hawklike, not Scandinavian. And it was draped in ecclesiastical robes rather than the tight-fitting military fashions favored by Axel.

After a few more steps I recognized the man. I recognized him even though it had been awhile since we had exchanged any words with each other. It was my former lover, Louis de Rohan.

Fortune had smiled on him since his return to Versailles as grand almoner. The people rightly blamed the crown for the economic mess the country was in and looked to the church for redemption of their wretchedness. Charismatic and popular, de Rohan came to symbolize churchly opposition to the throne in the masses' eyes.

This had given him leverage at Versailles, leverage he was quick to turn to his own advantage, leverage that translated into power. Soon the government was divided between the followers of the King and the followers of the cleric. Pressure was exerted to have him appointed Cardinal of all France, a position second in Christendom only to that of the Pope, and traditionally quite independent of Rome. In 1778 King Louis had succumbed to that pressure and my former lover was indeed appointed Cardinal Rohan. Since that time he had been consolidating his position with all of the considerable influence he could command.

The most significant influence he could not command

made her sit astride me, facing, and bounced her just as the old King used to bounce me. I could sense her pussy becoming more and more inflamed as it rubbed over my leg.

When I released Yolande, she slipped away from the dice game with her lover. Deliberately winking at Axel, I put my arms around a young lady-in-waiting and a pink-cheeked lieutenant of the Swiss Guards. I pulled them close together with myself in the middle and then I took his hand and placed it inside her bodice and I took her hand and placed it between his legs. "You two have won enough of my money," I announced. "Now go somewhere and make love. It really can be more fun than gambling, I am told."

The general laugh, I fear, was in response to my last three words and at the expense of my husband, the King.

I held out my goblet to be filled. Alas, the champagne was no longer flowing. The wine steward had retired for the night. We were quite out of the bubbly.

"I am the Queen and I am the great provider," I announced a bit tipsily. "I will replenish the supply."

Several young men got to their feet and offered to accompany me on this mission. I declined their offers, telling them that my destination was a royal secret and that I must go alone. "But," I whispered to Axel Fersen as I brushed past him, "I could be followed."

My heart was pounding in anticipation of his acting on this suggestion as I exited the palace and crossed the formal gardens to the road leading to the Petit Trianon. My little playhouse had a wine cellar, and I, of course, had a key to it. There was always a more than adequate stock of vintage champagne stored there. But the wine was only the excuse for my mission. The opportunity to